Signature Tastes
of
ATLANTA

SMOKE ALARM

MEDIA

For my grandmother, Mrs. Ruth Meadows Siler, the Last Queen. Anything great that I might accomplish in this world is simply a reflection of your influence.

To the restaurants, for making these incredible recipes available, and constantly improving them so that we can do a second edition.

Welcome to Atlanta: Phoenix from the Ashes photography from Wikipedia and the Atlanta History Center.

To others unnamed, because my memory is as short as my hair.

You can find us at www.signaturetastes.com and on Facebook: Signature Tastes

Layout by Steven W. Siler

Photography by Rosalie Freudes and team, except where noted

Siler, Steven W.

Signature Tastes of Atlanta: Favorite Recipes from our Local Restaurants

ISBN 978-1-927458-05-1

1. Restaurants Georgia-Atlanta-Guidebooks. 2. Cookery Georgia-Atlanta

Printed in the United States of America

This book is dedicated to the emergency responders...

From the first frantic call to 9-1-1
To the comforting hands at the Emergency Department
You give your time...

away from spouses,
away from friends,
away from children,
And yes, even from meals...

To assure all of us:

"Tonight, I will make it better for you
no matter what,
I will watch over you..."

W. Peachtree St NE

Peachtree St NE

Peachtree St NW

I have always wondered if anyone really reads the Table of Contents. Now since this is a cookbook, I should have organized everything under its proper heading, like soups, pasta, desserts and the like. This is not just a cookbook as much as a Culinary Postcard; a celebration of the city itself...about the eateries, fine dining, casual dining, bars, drive -ins, and of course, the people.

Signature Tastes of ATLANTA

Welcome to Atlanta: Phoenix Rising from the Ashes 7

The Eateries...

"Coming from a small town, it was tough to dream big. When I grew up in a small town in Georgia, my biggest dream was one day to be able to go to Atlanta..."

Herschel Walker, UGA and NFL Star

Welcome to Atlanta! Atlanta is the capital of the state of Georgia, and its most populous city. It is the fifth city to act as Georgia's capital, after letting Savannah, Augusta, Louisville, and Milledgeville have a try. The Atlanta metropolitan area is home to nearly 5,300,000 people, making it the ninth largest in the US, and Geor-

gia's cultural and economic center. If you are visiting, you're in good company; Atlanta is the seventh most visited city in the country, with visitors numbering over 35 million each year – clearly there is something to the notion of Southern hospitality.

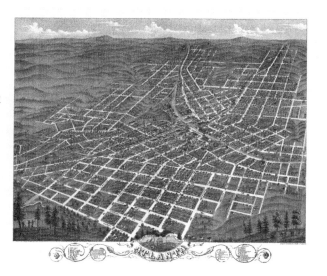

Like many US cities, Atlanta started out as a small settlement along a railroad line –in 1836, the Georgia General Assembly decided to build a railroad that would provide a route for trade to the Midwest; in 1837 the terminus was chosen, and over

the next few years people began building houses, a general store, and establishing a small settlement. By 1842, that settlement – which was already being called Atlanta – had 30 residents, living in 6 freshly-constructed houses. Then, in 1845 – after spending 1843-1844 trying out the name Marthasville – the city of Atlanta was incorporated. Within the next decade, four additional rail lines were running through the city, making it the railway hub of the Southern US.

It also holds the dubious distinction of being the only North American city to ever have fire used against it as an act of war; in 1864, during the Civil War, General Sherman had the city burned, successfully destroying most of the buildings from that era. However, Atlanta made a quick recovery after the Civil War, and to this

BURNING OF THE RAILROAD ROUND-HOUSE AT ATLANTA, NOVEMBER 14th, 1864 — FEDERAL SOLDIERS AT WORK ALONG THE RAILROAD TRACK.

day its symbol is the Phoenix, the mythological bird that rises from its own ashes, reborn. These days, the city is the Southeastern United States' main transportation hub – via highway, railroad, and air – and the Hartsfield-Jackson Atlanta International Airport has ranked as one of the world's busiest since 1998.

Atlanta has one of the top economic ratings in the US, and is a home to business, finance, and IT, as well as important services, government, and education. It is also home to the world headquarters of such companies as The Home Depot, UPS, Turner Broadcasting, Delta Airlines, and The Coca-Cola Company – in fact, Pemberton Place, the location of New World of Coca-Cola, is named after Atlanta pharmacist Dr. John Smith Pemberton, the man who first produced Coca-Cola syrup in 1886,

CHRONOLOGY OF THE GLASS PACKAGE FOR COCA-COLA
1894 ------ 1975

1894 1899–1902 1900 ----- 1916 1915 Nov. 16

and had it sold at the soda fountain in the pharmacy down the street for a nickel a glass soon after.

Part of the city's swift recovery from its Civil War wounds is due to its attempts to identify as the "New South" – shifting the focus from agriculture and traditional "Old South" political attitudes, and moving toward a more modern future. It worked — the Georgia School of Technology, now called the Georgia Institute of Technology — or simply, Georgia Tech — was founded in 1885; the Atlanta skyline began to feature skyscrapers as early as

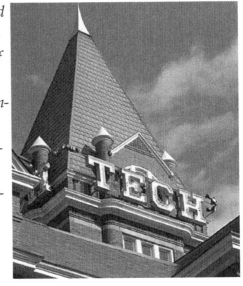

1892 — with the Equitable Building — and by the beginning of the 20th century, Atlanta was firmly established as a center of business in the American South. Its look has always been more modern and streamlined than that of many of its Southern neighbors. It didn't begin as a rich upper-class town, and after being burned down during the Civil War, any antebellum architecture it had was destroyed. And so, the city is filled with modern and post-modern structures by some of the 20th century's most prominent architects, which include many mid-to-high rise buildings in its commercial areas. Notably,

Atlanta's Bank of America Plaza ranks as the 9th tallest skyscraper in the United States.

Georgia is famous for its peaches, and if you spend any time exploring its capital, you will notice the same street signs appearing over and over again — there are, in fact, 55 *different Peachtree streets in Atlanta! Surprisingly, not a single one is actually named for peaches – they all come from the original inhabitants of the area, the Cherokee and Creek Indian nations. One of the largest Creek settlements featured a single, tall tree, referred to as "Standing Pitch Tree." After enough time, "pitch" turned into "peach." However, if you're in Atlanta during peach season, that shouldn't stop you from eating as many ripe peaches as you possibly can; the city has many farmers markets*

that are bursting with fresh, locally-grown produce – and several of the markets, including the Decatur and the Morningside, are strictly organic – offering handmade pickles, preserves, cheeses, and more. Georgia is also known for peanuts and

pecans – you'll find plenty of both in its markets, ready to be taken home as delicious souvenirs – a sweet slice of fresh-baked pecan pie is an excellent way to finish off a lazy evening meal.

Grits – a dish made from cornmeal with an infinite number of variations depending on who is preparing it – is Georgia's state dish. You'll find them on menus everywhere, and you should definitely give them a try. In addition to fried chicken, seafood, chicken and dumplings, Brunswick stew, fresh corn on the cob, and cornbread – Atlanta also loves its barbeque – and when it comes to barbeque in Georgia, pork is king. There are barbeque festivals that take place at various times during the year and plenty of restaurants offer their special recipes. Georgia is so fond of barbeque that the Georgia General Assembly holds an event called a "wild hog supper" before its legislative sessions.

Looking for something a little less Southern? Not to worry – Atlanta also has a wide range of more international food experiences; check out Buford Highway, a long road full of small, family-owned ethnic restaurants from all corners of the globe.

Street food is also a growing trend in the city, and you'll find a variety of food trucks serving up all kinds of goodies – in fact, every Friday, many of the city's food trucks converge along 17½ Street, offering a range of picnic-lunch options. You'll find everything from Korean BBQ to old fashioned mac n' cheese, and just about everything in between. Atlanta also has many different festivals during the year in its many public parks – the Ice Cream Festival held in Piedmont Park in August or early autumn's JapanFest are the perfect way to relax after a visit to some of the city's historical sites, like the Jimmy Carter Presidential Library and Museum or the Martin Luther King Jr. Historical Site. Atlanta is one of only two cities in the world to have been home to two Nobel Peace Prize award-winners, so don't miss the opportunity to take a look at the sites honoring these two important figures of US history.

If you are craving a healthy dose of history, modernity, and all points in between, along with some good old-fashioned Southern cooking and charm – and an ice-cold glass of Coca-Cola to wash it all down – Atlanta might be exactly what you've been looking for.

RECIPES & RESTAURANTS

North Georgia Apple and Crispy Brussels Sprouts Salad

Crispy fried Brussels sprouts, crisp tart apples and pistachios … who would have thunk it would taste so good? Well, the folks at 4th & Swift thought so, and many of their customers agree. This recipe proves, once and for all, that absolutely everything tastes better deep fried. And served with heavy cream. "They're crispy and have such nice flavor," said proprietor Jay Swift, who credits chef de partie Sal Purpura with creating the recipe.

2½ C. apple cider
½ C. shelled raw pistachios
1 sprig rosemary, stem removed, leaves finely chopped
1 pinch fleur de sel
vegetable oil for frying
26 Brussels sprouts, trimmed and cut in half
2 tbsp. sherry vinegar
salt and pepper
½ C. crème fraîche
2 tart apples, such as Granny Smith, peeled, quartered, cored and thinly sliced

1. In a small pot over high heat, boil cider until it is reduced to a thin syrup, about 30 minutes. (You should have approximately ¼ cup.) Set aside to cool.

2. Meanwhile, in a small ungreased pan set over low heat, toast the pistachios, stirring occasionally, about 10 minutes. Remove from pan to cool then chop coarsely. Combine the chopped pistachios with the rosemary leaves and fleur de sel. Set aside.

3. In a heavy pot or fryer, heat the oil to 350°F. Fry the Brussels sprout halves until the outside leaves begin to turn golden brown. Do not overfry or they will turn mushy. Remove the sprouts from the oil and toss in a bowl with the sherry vinegar and a dash each of salt and pepper.

4. Set out four plates and spread 2 tbsp. crème fraîche in a line on each plate. Arrange 6 or 7 sprout halves over the crème fraîche. Divide the apples evenly among the plates. Drizzle the cider reduction over the apples and Brussels sprouts and then sprinkle each salad with the pistachio-rosemary mixture. Serve immediately.

621 North Ave. N.E., B100

4TH & SWIFT

"The sweeter the apple, the blacker the core. Scratch a lover and find a foe!"
Dorothy Parker

Blue Cheese Potato Chips

Anton Uys, manager-owner of the Cabbagetown restaurant 97 Estoria, shared an industrial secret in the preparation of these chips: Soaking the potatoes in a solution of water and baking soda not only keeps them from discoloring, but it also "drops the starch so they don't come up really glassy," he said. The result: crisp, light chips that are the perfect foil to the creamy, tangy dressing.

2½ lb. Yukon Gold potatoes
1 tbsp. baking soda
1 tbsp. finely chopped, oil-packed, sun-dried tomatoes
1½ tsp. garlic powder
2 tbsp. plus ½ C. blue cheese crumbles, divided
½ C. mayonnaise
3 tbsp. half and half
2 tbsp. buttermilk
vegetable oil for frying
salt, to taste
½ C. diced tomatoes
¼ C. chopped green onions

1. Rinse, but do not peel, potatoes. Using a mandoline or a sharp knife, thinly slice potatoes—you do not want them paper-thin, but thin enough to cook up crisply.

2. Fill a large bowl with cold water and stir in the baking soda. Add sliced potatoes and allow to soak for 2 hours in the refrigerator.

3. Meanwhile, prepare the dressing. In a small bowl, combine the tomatoes, garlic powder, 2 tablespoons blue cheese crumbles, mayonnaise, half and half and buttermilk. Whisk until well-combined; refrigerate until needed.

4. Remove the potatoes from the water and pat dry on paper towels.

5. Heat the oil in a heavy pot or fryer to 375°F.

6. Preheat the broiler. Fry the potatoes until crisp and golden brown. Drain on paper towels and sprinkle lightly with salt.

7. Arrange chips in an ovenproof serving dish. Drizzle with the dressing and sprinkle with remaining ½ cup blue cheese crumbles.

8. Broil for 2 to 3 minutes, until bubbly.

9. Remove chips from the oven and top with tomatoes and green onions. Serve immediately.

97 Estoria
727 Wylie St

"A diet that consists predominantly of rice leads to the use of opium, just as a diet that consists predominantly of potatoes leads to the use of liquor."
Friedrich Nietzsche

Signature Taste of ATLANTA

6 oz. grouper, diced
2 tbsp. butter
½ bunch green onions, sliced thinly
1 large egg
1 tsp. salt, or more to taste
1 tbsp. Dijon mustard
5 dashes Tabasco sauce
5 dashes Worcestershire sauce
1 C. heavy cream
1 lb. jumbo lump crab meat, cleaned of all shell and cartilage

1. Place the grouper and the blade and bowl of a food processor in the freezer to chill for 20 minutes.

2. Meanwhile, in a small skillet, melt the butter over medium heat and cook the green onions until just wilted. Set aside to cool to room temperature.

3. Remove grouper and food processor pieces from freezer. Place grouper in the processor bowl and puree on high about 1 minute.

4. Scrape down the bowl with a rubber spatula. Add the egg and process the mixture until smooth and shiny.

5. Scrape down the bowl again and add the salt, Dijon mustard, Tabasco and Worcestershire. Process until incorporated.

6. With the machine running, add the heavy cream in a slow, steady stream until incorporated. The mixture should be light and fluffy.

7. Preheat oven to 425°F.

8. Fold crab and green onions into the fish mousse. Place four 3-inch metal ring molds on a lightly oiled nonstick ovenproof pan and fill with the crab mixture.

9. In an ovenproof skillet, sauté crab cakes over medium heat until lightly browned on each side, about 3 minutes per side.

10. Remove rings and place pan in oven. Bake for 12 to 16 minutes, until springy to the touch.

11. Serve with lobster sauce and seasonal lettuces.

103 WEST PACES FERRY ROAD

103 WEST

"The crab cakes with the walnuts and blue cheese go together nicely"
Linda Pierce

HONEY AND CIDER COLLARD GREENS

Greens of some sort have always been on the menu at Agave, said managing partner Tim Pinkham, but ever since chef Richard Silvey and owner Jack Sobel created their honey and cider collards about two years ago, the restaurant hasn't tampered with success. "They've become just one of our signature dishes," Pinkham said. "We don't dare take it off so we don't aggravate our clientele." It's the magic trio of honey, apple cider vinegar and apple-wood-smoked bacon that thrills diners, added sous chef Shawn Herrick. "That's pretty much why they rave about them."

1 smoked ham hock
3 large yellow onions, divided
3 whole bay leaves
1 gallon water
1 large bunch collard greens, washed, stems removed, chopped into strips
8 oz. apple-wood-smoked bacon, cut into ¼-in. pieces
¼ C. minced garlic
½ C. honey
1 C. apple cider vinegar
1 tbsp. salt (or to taste)
1 tsp. freshly ground black pepper (or to taste)

1. In a large pot, boil ham hock, 1 onion, roughly chopped, and the bay leaves in 1 gallon water for 1 hour. Remove the bay leaves and add the collard greens.

2. Dice the remaining 2 onions into ¼-inch pcs. In a separate large pan over medium-high heat, sauté the bacon until crispy, about 5 minutes, then add the onions and garlic.

3. When the onions begin to brown, add the honey, vinegar, salt and pepper. Simmer for 2 to 3 minutes, then add the mixture to the pot with the collards.

4. Cook for about 2 hours over a slow simmer, until collards are tender but not too soft, adding water as necessary. Cool slightly before serving.

242 BOULEVARD S.E.

AGAVE

"Hope is the only bee that makes honey without flowers."
Robert Green Ingersoll

23

Alfredo's

Italian Restaurant

Regional Italian Cuisine

1974
Established

RICOTTA CHEESECAKE

Signature Tastes of ATLANTA

1 tbsp. butter, softened
2 tbsp. all-purpose flour
7 eggs
4 lbs. whole milk ricotta cheese
½ C. dark crème de cacao
2 tbsp. vanilla
3 C. granulated sugar
1 C. chocolate chips

1. Preheat oven to 350°F. Lightly butter and flour a 10-inch springform pan, shaking out any excess. Set aside.

2. In a very large bowl, beat the eggs.

3. Add ricotta, crème de cacao and vanilla and fold until well combined.

4. Add sugar and fold again. Add chocolate chips and fold until evenly distributed.

5. Transfer batter to pan.

6. Place springform pan in a large roasting pan and add enough tap water to come ¼ of the way up the pan.

7. Bake for 2½ hours, or until golden and the edges are firm but center moves slightly when shaken gently.

8. Cool for 4 hours before serving.

ALFREDO'S
4058 PEACHTREE ROAD

"I argued that I didn't have any of the attributes to pose for cheesecake. I said I would have to make good on my acting ability, which was the only attribute I could offer."
Teresa Wright

PANNA COTTA

Antica Posta offers quintessential Tuscan cooking. Open nightly for dinner, the exhibition kitchen features Tuscan specialties, signature meat and fish dishes, homemade pastas and breads, and delicious appetizers. Antica Posta's cozy dining rooms and elegant bar and lounge beckon diners to experience a touch of Tuscany nestled in the archetype Buckhead!

1 envelope (2¼ tsp.) unflavored gelatin
½ to ¾ C. cold water
4 C. heavy cream
½ vanilla bean
⅔ C. granulated sugar
2 C. pureed berries
1 C. diced pineapple
10 raspberries
10 mint leaf sprigs

1. Lightly grease 10 (6-8-oz.) ramekins.

2. In a bowl, dissolve gelatin in cold water.

3. In a saucepan, gently heat cream with vanilla bean to a light boil.

4. Remove from heat and add sugar and gelatin mixture, stirring well to combine.

5. Remove the vanilla bean. Pour mixture into ramekins and refrigerate for 6 hours or overnight, until set.

6. Invert molds on to individual serving plates (if molds are hard to dislodge, run a knife around the sides or heat the bottom of the mold for 5 seconds).

7. Drizzle berry puree over panna cotta. Garnish each with pineapple, raspberry and a mint leaf.

ANTICA POSTA
519 E. Paces Ferry Road N.E.

"The friendly cow all red and white, I love with all my heart: She gives me cream with all her might; to eat with apple tart."
Robert Louis Stevenson

ORANGE POUNDCAKE

Signature Tastes of ATLANTA

For the Orange Poundcake:
1 lb. (4 sticks) unsalted butter, at room temperature
1¼ C. granulated sugar, divided
grated zest from 1 navel orange
3 tbsp. freshly squeezed orange juice
5 eggs, separated
3 C. cake flour
heaping ¼ tsp. salt
heaping ¼ tsp. baking soda
¾ C. buttermilk
2 tbsp. butter, softened (optional)

For the Lemon Sauce:
1⅔ C. granulated sugar
¾ C. freshly squeezed lemon juice
3 whole eggs
1 C. (2 sticks) unsalted butter, cut into small pcs., at room temperature

For the Orange Poundcake:
1. Preheat oven to 350°F. Lightly grease a loaf pan.
2. In the bowl of a mixer fitted with a paddle attachment, place the butter, 1 cup sugar, orange zest and juice; cream for 5 minutes, scraping the sides of the bowl and beater occasionally. Add the egg yolks slowly, scraping the bowl between additions.
3. In a separate bowl, sift together the flour, salt and baking soda. Gradually add to the butter mixture, alternating with the buttermilk, just until incorporated. Set aside.
4. In a bowl of a mixer fitted with a whisk attachment, add the egg whites and whip until frothy. With the mixer running, add the remaining ¼ cup sugar gradually. Continue whipping until the whites reach soft peaks.
5. Slowly and gently fold the whites into the batter until fully incorporated. Scrape the batter evenly into the loaf pan, and immediately place in the hot oven.
6. Bake for 40 minutes without opening the oven. After 40 minutes, check the cake with a bamboo skewer; if the skewer comes out clean, the cake is ready. If not, bake for 5 to 10 minutes, and check again. Cool the finished cake for 10 minutes, then turn the pan over onto a clean surface and let cool fully.
7. Slice the cake, lightly butter each piece and toast in a 350°F oven until browned. Top with 2 tablespoons of lemon sauce, or to taste.

For the Lemon Sauce:
1. In a stainless steel bowl over a pot of simmering water, place the sugar and lemon juice and heat until the sugar melts, whisking frequently.
2. In a separate bowl, whip the eggs lightly.
3. When the sugar and lemon juice are hot, gradually pour a few tablespoons over the eggs, whisking constantly to warm eggs and incorporate the mixture. Replace over the simmering water, cooking until thick (it will coat the back of a spoon), using a rubber spatula to stir occasionally.
4. Remove from heat to cool slightly. Add the butter, whisking in a few pieces at a time, until a smooth mixture is achieved. Place a piece of plastic wrap directly over the mixture and place in the refrigerator until completely cooled.

490 E. PACES FERRY ROAD

ARIA

"When you squeeze an orange, orange juice comes out — because that's what's inside. When you are squeezed, what comes out is what is inside."
Wayne Dyer

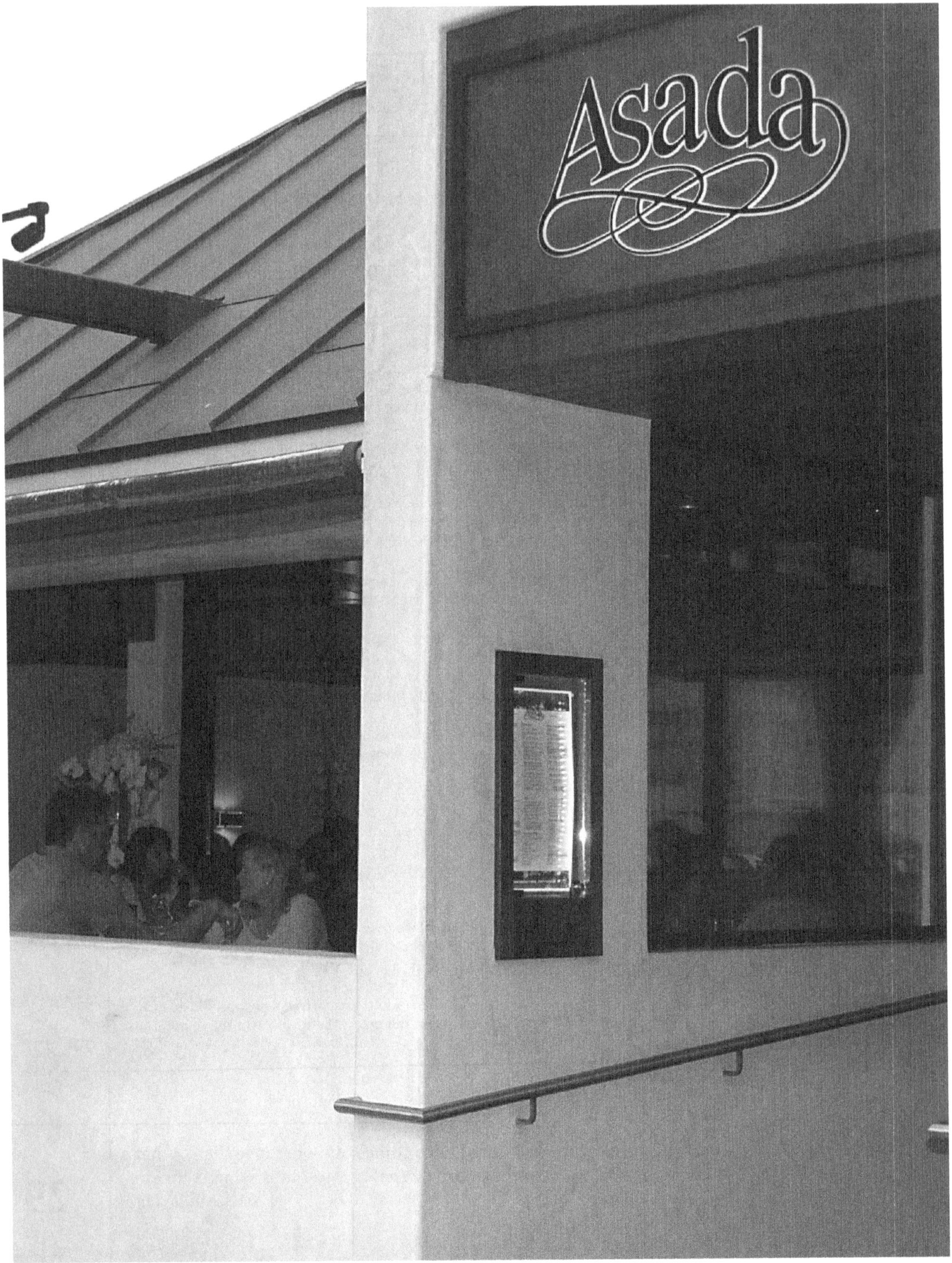
Asada

SPICY CHIPOTLE CREAM SAUCE WITH SEARED SEA SCALLOPS

Co-owner Liz Callison describes this creation by her partner, chef Michael Hosp, as almost druglike: "At first you say, 'Oh my God, it's hot!' But then before you know it, you're craving the next bite."

Signature Tastes of ATLANTA

1 (7-oz.) can chipotle peppers in adobo sauce
½ lb. dried linguine
2 tbsp. olive oil
12 dry-packed sea scallops (about ¾ lb.)
salt and freshly ground white pepper
4 cloves garlic, minced
½ C. dry white wine
1 C. heavy cream
2 tbsp. freshly grated parmesan cheese
dried red pepper flakes, to taste

1. Empty the can of chipotle peppers into a blender or food processor and puree. Set aside 1 to 2 tablespoons of the puree for the sauce; save the remaining puree for another use.

2. Bring a large pot of salted water to boil for the pasta. Cook the pasta al dente; drain.

3. While the pasta cooks, prepare the scallops. Heat olive oil in a medium sauté pan over medium-high heat. Season scallops with salt and pepper and add to the pan. Sear on one side for about 1 minute and turn.

4. Add 1 to 2 tablespoons of chipotle puree and the chopped garlic and toss. Add white wine to deglaze the pan.

5. When liquid has been reduced by half, add the cream. Cook on high until the sauce is slightly thickened, about 5 minutes. Remove scallops from pan and set aside. Add the cooked linguine to the pan and toss with the sauce.

6. Transfer to a serving bowl and arrange the scallops on top. Garnish with parmesan cheese and dried red pepper flakes.

1238 DEKALB AVE.

ASADA

"With scallops, it's where you get them. We get them live in the shell. I'm willing to share our connection with the White House. This could be the start of a beautiful love affair with the scallop."
Eric Ripert

SOUTHERN FRIED CHICKEN

Signature Taste of ATLANTA

Atkins Park Tavern Restaurant Group was conceived by Warren Bruno in 1983 and is now owned and operated by his wife, Sandra Spoon, friend Kevin Drawe and the management staff of the individual restaurants. An Atlanta legend, the original Atkins Park Tavern Restaurant enjoys a colorful history as Atlanta's oldest continuously-licensed tavern. What began as a deli in 1922 is now a smart-casual restaurant that offers upscale comfort cuisine. The Atkins Park Tavern Restaurant Group offers family dining, weekend brunch, private party facilities, and late-night drinks. Visit us in Smyrna and the original location in Virginia Highland.

For the Fried Chicken:
4 (6-oz.) boneless chicken breasts
2 to 3 C. buttermilk, divided
vegetable oil for frying
2 C. all-purpose flour
1 tsp. salt
½ tsp. ground black pepper

For the Sawmill Gravy:
2 tbsp. bacon grease
2½ tbsp. all-purpose flour
1 C. whole milk
¼ tsp. ground black pepper (or to taste)
salt, to taste

For the Fried Chicken:

1. Place the chicken in a plastic storage container and pour enough buttermilk over the chicken to cover (about 1 cup). Turn the chicken to make sure it is completely covered in buttermilk. Cover the container and store in the refrigerator overnight.

2. Heat the vegetable oil in a fryer or heavy pan to 350°F.

3. In a mixing bowl, combine the flour, salt and pepper. In another bowl add about 1 cup buttermilk. Remove the chicken pieces from the soaking buttermilk (discard this liquid) and shake off the excess buttermilk.

4. Roll each piece of chicken in the flour to coat, then dip in the fresh buttermilk to coat, then roll again in the flour to completely coat.

5. Fry the chicken in the hot oil until brown and crispy on the outside and cooked through, 10-15 minutes. Drain the chicken on paper towels. Serve hot with Sawmill Gravy.

For the Gravy:
1. In a small saucepan over medium heat, melt the bacon grease. Stir in the flour and cook, stirring regularly for 2-3 minutes. Slowly whisk in the milk and cook, whisking until mixture comes to a simmer and gravy thickens.

2. Stir in the pepper and season to taste with salt and additional pepper, if desired.

ATKINS PARK TAVERN
794 N HIGHLAND AVENUE NORTHEAST

"Business is never so healthy as when, like a chicken, it must do a certain amount of scratching of what it gets"
Henry Ford

Hong Kong-Style Fish

Executive chef Robert Holley describes Hong Kong-Style Fish as one of Atlanta Fish Market's signature dishes. Steamed fish fillets and sautéed spinach sit in an Asian-flavored broth. Garnished with julienned fresh ginger and green onions, this dish has a great combination of flavors and textures.

½ C. low-sodium soy sauce
¼ C. water
3 oz. dry sherry
2 tbsp. granulated sugar
2 tbsp. sesame oil
2 tbsp. olive oil
1 lb. fresh spinach, washed and stemmed
freshly ground black pepper
2 (6-oz.) white fish filets
2 tbsp. finely julienned ginger
2 tbsp. finely julienned green onions

1. In a saucepan, combine soy sauce, water, sherry and sugar and bring to a boil. Reduce heat to low to keep warm.

2. In a large skillet, heat sesame and olive oils. Add spinach and toss until wilted. Season with pepper and set aside.

3. Steam or sauté fish until just done. Do not overcook.

4. To assemble: In a large soup bowl, place a bed of spinach. Rest fish on top of spinach and garnish with ginger and green onions. Pour soy broth over fish and serve.

ATLANTA FISH MARKET
265 PHARR ROAD

"No human being, however great, or powerful, was ever so free as a fish."
John Ruskin

SAGE SAUCE

Atmosphere celebrated it's eighth anniversary in March of 2010 and has received such prestigious awards as Atlanta's Best French Restaurant from Creative Loafing and Citysearch. With a cuisine based on the traditional French foods with a modern twist, you will finally discover a place that is not just trendy! Set in a beautiful, restored home built in the mid 50's, Atmosphere is warm and inviting – casual yet elegant. We are open for lunch Tuesday through Friday and brunch on Saturday and Sunday of each week and offer dinner every day of the week but Monday. We welcome large parties and have a private dining area to entertain up to 20 guests.

½ C. unsalted butter, divided
3 shallots, peeled and sliced
2 garlic cloves, peeled and sliced
3 tbsp. tomato paste
2 C. white wine
2 C. veal stock, prepared from concentrate
6 fresh sage leaves
8 Niçoise olives

1. In a saucepan over medium-low heat, melt 2 tbsp. of butter.

2. Add the shallots and garlic and sauté until soft, about 2-3 minutes.

3. Add the tomato paste and cook for 5 minutes, stirring frequently. Add the white wine, stirring well. Increase heat to medium high, and cook until liquid has reduced and thickened.

4. Add the veal stock and cook, stirring occasionally, until liquid is reduced by half.

5. Add the sage leaves, cover the pot and turn off the heat. Let the leaves steep for 5 minutes.

6. Strain through a fine mesh strainer. Set aside until ready to serve.

7. Before serving, return sauce to saucepan over medium heat. Stir in remaining 2 tbsp. butter and add olives. Swirl in the pan until the butter is melted and the sauce has a shiny glaze.

ATMOSPHERE
1620 PIEDMONT AVE.

"The sage does not hoard. The more he helps others, the more he benefits himself, The more he gives to others, the more he gets himself. The Way of Heaven does one good but never does one harm. The Way of the sage is to act but not to compete."
Lao Tzu

KEY LIME TART

Bacchanalia is Atlanta's most celebrated restaurant featuring contemporary American cuisine from chefs/owners Anne Quatrano and Clifford Harrison. Expect incredibly fresh and flavorful choices with masterful preparation and presentation. Bacchanalia's seasonal menu relies entirely on organic ingredients, many sourced from Anne and Clifford's farm, so that diners can have an utterly unique dining experience each time they return. The menu can also be ordered à la carte at the bar.

For the Ginger Snaps:
3¾ C. all-purpose flour
2 tbsp. ground ginger
1 tbsp. ground cinnamon
1¼ tsp. baking powder
½ tsp. ground white pepper
¼ tsp. ground cloves
1¾ C. packed dark brown sugar
1½ C. (3 sticks) unsalted butter, softened
1 egg
1 tbsp. grated fresh ginger
1½ tsp. lemon zest
4 tbsp. butter, melted

For the Filling:
6 egg yolks
2 cans sweetened condensed milk
1 C. Key lime juice
zest of 2 key limes

For the Meringue:
6 egg whites
1 tsp. cream of tartar
1 C. granulated sugar

To Prepare the Ginger Snaps:
1. In a bowl, combine flour, ground ginger, cinnamon, baking powder, pepper and cloves. Set aside.
2. With an electric mixer, beat brown sugar and 1½ cups butter until smooth. Add the egg, fresh ginger and lemon zest and beat until combined.
3. Gradually add dry ingredients, beating until well-combined. Turn out dough into plastic wrap and press into a thin disc. Refrigerate for 4 hours.
4. Preheat oven to 325°F.
5. Roll about ⅓ of the dough until about ¼ -inch thick. Cut dough into 2-by-2-inch cookies. Place cookies on parchment paper-lined baking sheets and bake for about 8 minutes, rotating once, until slightly brown. The cookies should be slightly overcooked for crispness. Set aside to cool on a rack. When cookies are completely cooled, process them in a food processor until finely ground.
6. Combine 2¼ cups cookie crumbs and melted butter. Press evenly into a 9-inch pie pan, going all the way up the sides. Set aside.

To Prepare the Filling:
1. Preheat oven to 300°F. With an electric mixer on high speed, beat egg yolks until pale and thickened, about 10 minutes. The yolks should fall like a ribbon from the beaters, and when dripped and should leave an impression for a few seconds before being absorbed.
2. Add sweetened condensed milk and beat well to combine. On low speed, add juice and zest.
3. Fill pie pan with filling just to the top of the crust. Bake for 20 minutes. Remove from oven, cool slightly, then refrigerate for 3 hours or overnight.
4. Right before serving, prepare meringue: On medium speed, beat egg whites until frothy. Add cream of tartar. Increase speed to high and slowly add sugar. Continue beating until whites are thick, glossy and fluffy.
5. Mound meringue on the pie. Using a hand-held torch, lightly brown meringue. Serve immediately.

BACCHANALIA
1198 HOWELL MILL ROAD

"I believe that if life gives you lemons, you should make lemonade... And try to find somebody whose life has given them vodka, and have a party."
Ron White

Before being a manager at Baraonda, I was a customer, and Penne Salsiccia was my favorite pasta dish," says Pietro Murganti. "It's a very rich and strongly flavorful dish." Customers tend to agree: "We know this because the plate is always empty, even though the portion is abundant," he says. It's also a very simple dish to prepare. It relies on good-quality ingredients, though, so look for top-notch fresh Italian sausage and imported cheese. This recipe was created as a dinner special at Baraonda three years ago by chef-owner Costanzo Astarita and chef Carlos Santizio. It has since become part of the regular menu. Murganti suggests pairing it with a chianti classico.

1 lb. penne rigate
1 lb. mild Italian sausage
1 lb. hot Italian sausage
2 tbsp. olive oil
3 shallots, peeled and thinly sliced
½ lb. button mushrooms, thinly sliced
salt and pepper, to taste
¼ C. white wine
3 C. heavy whipping cream
2 tbsp. chopped fresh parsley
¼ C. grated Grana Padano or Parmigiano-Reggiano cheese

1. Bring a large pot of salted water to boil. Cook the pasta until al dente. Drain, reserving some of the cooking water.

2. Meanwhile, remove the sausages from the casings and cook them in a large skillet over medium-high heat, breaking up the meat as it cooks. When the sausages are cooked through, transfer them to a strainer and let the fat run off. Wipe the skillet with a paper towel and return it to the heat.

3. Add the olive oil to the skillet and cook the shallots, stirring occasionally, until tender. Push the shallots aside and add the mushrooms. Sprinkle lightly with salt and pepper. Cook, stirring occasionally, until the mushrooms are reduced in size and most of the moisture is gone from the pan. Add the wine and cook until the liquid has evaporated.

4. Return the sausage to the pan with the shallots and mushrooms and add the cream. Bring the cream to a boil and cook, stirring occasionally, until it reduces by about half and is thick enough to cling to pasta. Toss with the drained pasta and add salt and pepper to taste. If the sauce is too thick, stir in a bit of the reserved pasta water. Sprinkle with parsley and cheese before serving.

BARAONDA
710 PEACHTREE ST. N.E.

"I do adore food. If I have any vice it's eating. If I was told I could only eat one food for the rest of my life, I could put up with sausage and mash forever."
Colin Baker

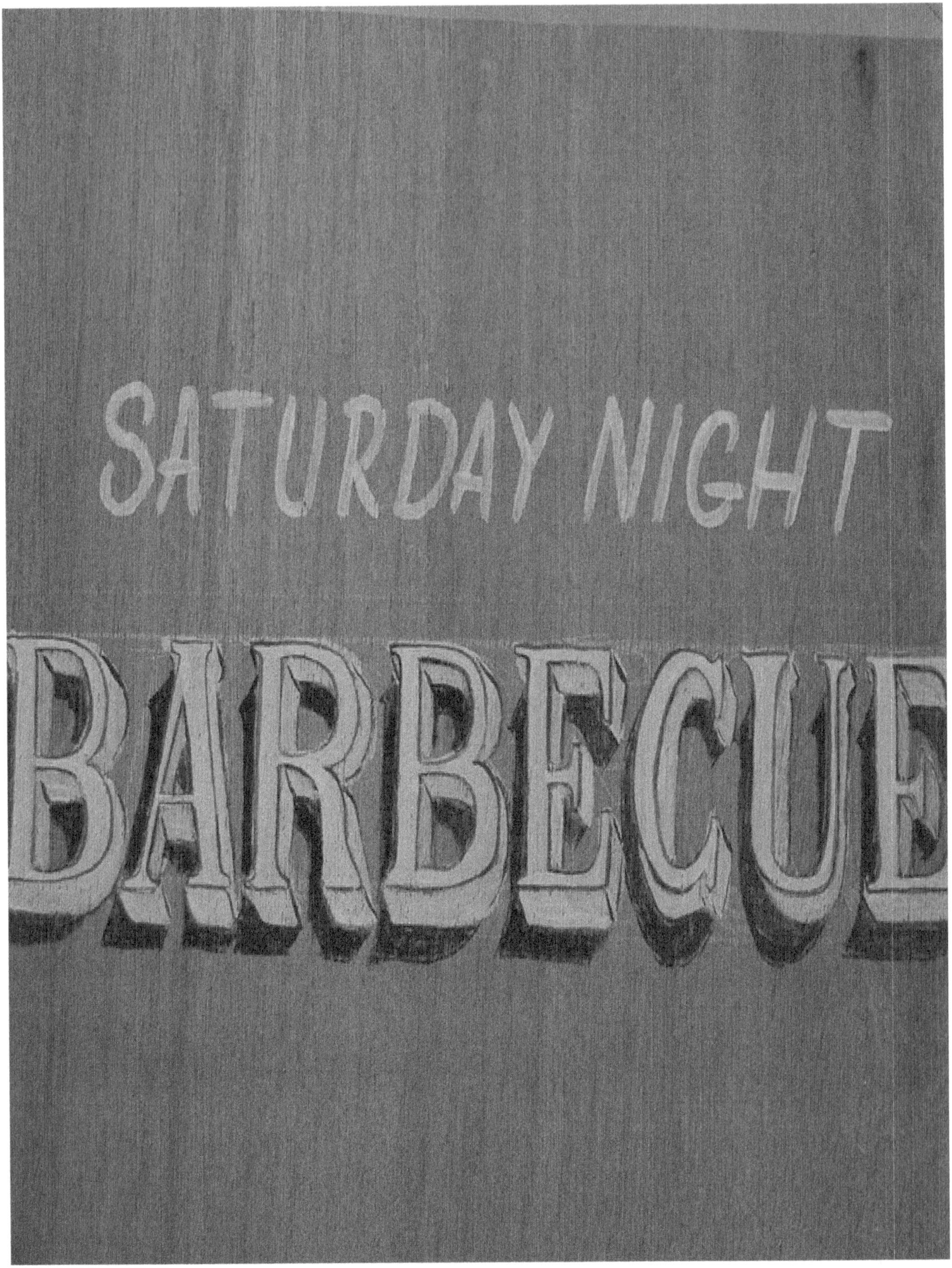
SATURDAY NIGHT
BARBECUE

Uncle Jeun's Coleslaw

Barbecue Works has the greatest tasting food of all of the Underground restaurants. For it to be "fast food" it really tastes like it just came out of my mom's kitchen. The best part is that the prices are crazy low. The food is just that good.

1 C. Miracle Whip
¼ C. granulated sugar
¼ tsp. Kosher salt
1 tbsp. apple cider vinegar
dash celery seed
dash ground black pepper
1 head green cabbage, quartered, cored and thinly sliced
1 medium carrot, julienned

1. In a large bowl, combine the Miracle Whip, sugar, salt, vinegar, celery seed and pepper, and stir until sugar is dissolved.

2. Add the cabbage and carrot and toss until the vegetables are evenly coated with the dressing.

BARBECUE WORKS
121 CENTRAL AVE. S.W.

"As far as the laws of barbecue refer to reality, they are not certain; and as far as they are certain, they do not refer to reality."
Albert Einstein

Yellow Squash Casserole

Warm and inviting like a centuries old cabin, the Blue Ridge Grill pays homage to the Blue Ridge Mountains. An immense stacked-stone fireplace, timbers rescued from an 1890's cotton mill, painted log walls and comfortable red leather booths create the unique combination of rustic, yet casual, elegance.

¼ C. olive oil
1 large yellow onion, sliced
4 large yellow squash, cut in half lengthwise and sliced in ¼-in. pieces
2 large zucchini, cut in half lengthwise and sliced in ¼-in. pieces
2 C. heavy cream
12 oz. grated cheddar cheese
4 C. Panko breadcrumbs
½ tbsp. salt
¼ tsp. white pepper
1 sleeve buttered crackers, crushed (about 36)
1 C. fried onions (optional)

1. Preheat oven to 350°F.

2. In a very large skillet or stockpot heat oil over medium-high heat.

3. Sauté onion, squash and zucchini for 3-5 minutes.

4. Add cream and bring to a simmer.

5. Stir in the cheese, breadcrumbs, salt and pepper. Stir until cheese melts and mixture is combined.

6. Transfer mixture to a baking dish. Sprinkle crushed crackers on top.

7. Bake 25 to 30 minutes. Garnish with fried onions if desired.

Blue Ridge Grill
1261 W. Paces Ferry Road

"If toast always lands butter-side down, and cats always land on their feet, what happens if you strap toast on the back of a cat and drop it?"
Stephen Wright

CRAB CAKES WITH WHOLE-GRAIN MUSTARD SAUCE

Kurt M. D'Aurizio, executive chef of Bold American Food Co., was happy to share his delicious version of crab cakes. He uses Panko, Japanese bread crumbs, to bind the patties and seasons them with a healthy dose of red pepper to give them a bit of heat.

Signature Tastes of ATLANTA

Whole-Grain Mustard Sauce:
¼ C. whole grain mustard
¼ C. mayonnaise
1 tbsp. dry white wine
salt and pepper

Crab Cakes:
¼ C. mayonnaise
¼ C. Panko breadcrumbs
1 tsp. thinly sliced green onions
½ tsp. cayenne pepper
½ tsp. paprika
¼ tsp. garlic powder
½ tsp. sea salt
¼ tsp. fresh ground pepper
1 lb. fresh lump crab meat
1 tbsp. vegetable oil

For the Whole-Grain Mustard Sauce:
1. In a bowl, combine mustard, mayonnaise and wine. Season to taste with salt and pepper and set aside.

For the Crab Cakes:
1. In a bowl, mix mayonnaise, Panko breadcrumbs, green onions, cayenne pepper, paprika, garlic powder, salt and pepper. Gently fold in crab meat, being careful not to break up the meat. Taste and adjust seasoning. Form into cakes.

2. In a large skillet, heat oil over medium-high heat. Sauté crab cakes until golden brown on both sides, flipping carefully to keep cakes intact. Serve with whole-grain mustard sauce.

BOLD AMERICAN FOOD CO.
887 WEST MARIETTA STREET NORTHWEST

"Love is like a mustard seed; planted by God and watered by men."
Muda Saint Michael

TEMPURA ALASKAN HALIBUT WITH SOY-CHILI GLAZE

Signature Tastes of ATLANTA

Soy-Chili Glaze:
1 (7-oz.) bottle sweet red chili sauce (like Thai Kitchen's Red Chili Dipping Sauce)
¼ C. low-sodium soy sauce
1 tsp. sesame oil
1 tsp. canola oil
1½ tbsp. orange juice
1 tsp. lemon juice
1 tsp. lime juice
½ tsp. Sriracha Chili Sauce (or other hot sauce), optional
½ tsp. chopped basil

Tempura Batter:
Canola or peanut oil
⅓ C. cornstarch
½ C. cake or all-purpose flour
½ to ¾ C. cold seltzer water
1 tbsp. salt
1 tsp. sesame oil
1 tbsp. sesame seeds

6 halibut fillets

1. In a bowl, whisk together sweet chili sauce, soy sauce, sesame oil, canola oil, orange juice, lemon juice, lime juice, chili sauce and basil until well-incorporated.

2. In a heavy pot, heat 3 inches of canola oil to 350°F.

3. To make the tempura batter, whisk together cornstarch and flour. Slowly whisk in seltzer water until batter is about the consistency of heavy cream. Add salt, sesame oil and sesame seeds.

4. Dip halibut fillets in batter, let excess drip off and slowly lower them, one by one, into the oil.

5. Fry 3 minutes per side; remove and drain briefly on paper towels. Serve with soy-chili glaze.

BROOKLYN CAFE
200 SANDY SPRINGS CIRCLE

"I couldn't believe it when I heard that vehicles run on tempura oil."
Ayako Fujii

49

PRETZEL BREAD

It was Pano Karatassos, the legendary Atlanta restauranteur and president and founder of Buckhead Life Restaurant Group, who conceived the idea of pretzel bread. He called upon Alou Niangadou, an award-winning bakery chef and executive bread baker at the Buckhead Bread Co., which provides bread for all the Buckhead Life restaurants as well as other top hotels and restaurants, to come up with such a creation.

3½ to 4 C. (1 lb.) high gluten or all-purpose flour
3 tbsp. granulated sugar, divided
1 tbsp. salt
2 (¼-oz.) packages active dry yeast
1 C. warm water (105 to 115°F)
½ C. (1 stick) butter, melted and cooled

Optional:
1 egg, beaten with 1 tbsp. water and 1 tsp. granulated sugar

1. Combine 3 cups of the flour, sugar and salt in a large mixing bowl.

2. In another bowl, dissolve the yeast in the warm water. Add cooled butter to the yeast mixture.

3. Add the butter-yeast mixture to the flour mixture in the large mixing bowl and stir to combine. Gradually add enough of the remaining flour to make a soft dough.

4. Turn dough out onto a lightly floured surface and knead until smooth. Place in a lightly greased bowl, cover bowl with a kitchen towel and let dough rise 30 minutes. Divide dough into 8 equal portions; shape into long bread sticks and place on baking sheets. Let rest 10 to 15 minutes while preheating oven to 350°F.

5. When oven is hot, brush optional egg glaze on bread sticks, sprinkle with additional sugar, if desired, and make slash marks using a very sharp knife across tops of bread sticks. Bake 20 to 30 minutes.

BUCKHEAD BREAD CO.
3070 PIEDMONT ROAD

"Enthusiasm is the yeast that raises the dough."
Paul J. Meyer

Spinach Ravioli with Roasted Tomatoes and Fried Eggplant

Café 640 has done well by focusing on what's good, what's seasonal, what's local... and what Chef Andy is excited about. Hence, the menu is quite eclectic, reflecting his French bistro experience from his time at Aria, along with some of his childhood favorites (try the Antipasto plate's Beet Deviled Egg, his grandmother's recipe). Year-round staples like Andy's Burger" – which, dare I say in this current era of burger-pandemonium – is one of the best I've had in a while; the delectable mussels, and a Panna Cotta that Andy claims is somewhat "underrated."

vegetable oil for frying
8 Roma tomatoes
2 tbsp. chopped fresh thyme
2 tbsp. olive oil
salt and pepper, to taste
4½ tbsp. unsalted butter, divided
2 tbsp. vegetable stock
1-2 tsp. freshly squeezed lemon juice
1 cup all-purpose flour
2 eggs
1½ C. fresh breadcrumbs
2 Chinese eggplants or 1 small regular eggplant, cut into 1-in. semicircles or wedges
24 spinach ravioli
¼ C. fresh chopped herbs (basil, thyme, parsley)
¼ C. shredded parmesan cheese

1. Preheat oven to 350°F. Bring a pot of salted water to boil. Preheat a fryer, or heat about 1-inch of vegetable oil in a small heavy pot for frying.

2. Cut tomatoes in half lengthwise. In a baking dish, toss the tomatoes with the thyme and olive oil; sprinkle with salt and pepper. Bake 10-15 minutes until the tomato skins start to peel off. Remove from the oven. Cool slightly, then remove the skins with a fork.

3. Meanwhile, in a small saucepan, slowly heat ½ tablespoon butter over medium-low heat. Cook, swirling occasionally, until the butter browns—but do not allow it to smoke or burn.

4. Add the vegetable stock and bring to a boil, then slowly whisk in the remaining 4 tablespoons butter until well-incorporated. Season to taste with the lemon juice, salt and pepper. Set aside.

5. Meanwhile, place the flour in a small bowl and season with salt and pepper. In a separate bowl, whisk the eggs with 2 tablespoons water. In a third bowl, place the breadcrumbs and season with salt and pepper.

6. Dredge the eggplant pieces in the flour, then dip in the egg wash and then toss with the breadcrumbs to coat. Don't worry if the crumbs don't stick to the skins of the eggplant; the exposed skins will add a splash of color to the completed dish.

7. Meanwhile, cook the ravioli in the boiling water until they float, 12-14 minutes. Drain and toss with all but 2 tablespoons of the lemon butter and with the chopped fresh herbs.

8. When the vegetable oil is heated to about 350°F, drop in the eggplant pieces and cook until browned and crispy, about 5-7 minutes. Drain on paper towels.

9. To arrange the dish, divide the ravioli among 4 plates. Top each with ¼ of the eggplant and the tomatoes (and juices). Drizzle with the remaining lemon butter and sprinkle with the parmesan cheese.

CAFE 640
640 N. Highland Ave.

"A world without tomatoes is like a string quartet without violins."
Laurie Colwin

WALNUT CHICKEN SALAD

Owner Johnny Liu was happy to share the recipe for his restaurant's best-selling item. Liu thinks it's the simplicity of the recipe that makes it such a hit. His secret is lots of chicken and not much else, just some golden raisins and chopped walnuts for flavor and texture.

1½ lb. skinless, boneless chicken breasts
½ C. chopped walnuts
⅓ C. golden raisins
3 to 4 tbsp. reduced-fat mayonnaise
1 tsp. salt
dash of black pepper

1. Gently poach chicken in water until it's just cooked through. Set aside to cool and then chop.

2. In a bowl, combine chicken, walnuts, raisins and enough mayonnaise to hold the salad together. Season with salt and pepper and stir well to combine.

CAFE AT PHARR
316 PHARR ROAD

"Love, like a chicken salad a restaurant has, must be taken with blind faith or it loses its flavor."
Helen Rowland

Café Intermezzo

Speisekarte

Cuisine

Das Europäische Kaffeehaus

Seit 1979

Moroccan Chickpea Soup

Café Intermezzo begun as an idea in the mind of Brian Olson, predicated upon his experience in, and love for, coffeehouses in Germany and Austria. Olson's partner in the opening of the Café, Renate Olson, grew-up in Hamburg, Germany, and spent many hours in Kaffeehausen. Their wish for a European coffeehouse to enjoy themselves promoted the opening of Café Intermezzo in the Atlanta suburb of Dunwoody on December 3, 1979. The eventual search for a second location yielded an excellent old building on Peachtree Street near Midtown Atlanta, which opened on December 29, 1987.

2 tbsp. olive oil
1 small onion, chopped
2 cloves garlic, minced
½ tsp. cinnamon
½ tsp. paprika
½ tsp. ground cumin
pinch cayenne pepper
1 (15-oz.) can diced tomatoes
2 (15-oz.) cans chickpeas, drained
3 C. vegetable broth
½ tsp. granulated sugar
salt and ground black pepper, to taste
4 C. packed fresh spinach, thinly sliced

1. In a large pot, heat olive oil over medium-high heat.

2. Add onion, garlic, cinnamon, paprika, cumin and cayenne. Cook, stirring occasionally, until onions are translucent, about 5 minutes.

3. Add tomatoes, chickpeas, vegetable broth and sugar. Simmer for 45 minutes.

4. Season to taste with salt and pepper.

5. To serve, divide spinach among 6 serving bowls. Ladle hot soup over the spinach.

CAFÉ INTERMEZZO
4505 ASHFORD DUNWOODY ROAD

"There is nothing like soup. It is by nature eccentric: no two are ever alike, unless of course you get your soup in a can."
Laurie Colwin

POTATO AND CAULIFLOWER SOUP

Cafe Sunflower appeals to people of all diets, and they return again and again for our delectable food, beautiful presentation, cozy atmosphere, and friendly service. We feature a wide variety of vegetarian dishes that incorporate elements from the Caribbean, Asia, the American Southwest, and the Mediterranean. Come join us, and taste for yourself!

Signature Tastes of ATLANTA

2 tbsp. olive oil
1 C. onion, diced
1 C. celery, diced
½ C. carrots, diced
2 cloves garlic, chopped
1 tsp. fresh dill, chopped
½ tsp. fresh thyme leaves
1½ C. cauliflower florets
4 C. vegetable stock
2 C. potatoes, peeled and chopped
2 bay leaves
salt and white pepper, to taste

1. In a large saucepan, heat the oil and sauté the onion, celery, carrots, garlic, dill and thyme for 5-7 minutes, or until tender and translucent.

2. Add cauliflower and cook 2-3 minutes. Add stock and potatoes, cover and cook on medium heat for 20-30 minutes until tender, stirring occasionally. Remove from heat.

3. In a blender, puree half the soup. Return the puree to the soup pot and add bay leaves and season with salt and white pepper. Simmer on low heat, uncovered, for 15-20 minutes, stirring occasionally.

CAFE SUNFLOWER
2140 PEACHTREE ROAD

"Explaining something sensible to Lord Killanin is akin to explaining something to a cauliflower. The advantage of the cauliflower is that if all else fails, you can always cover it with melted cheese and eat it."
William E. Simon

Canoe pastry chef Robyn Mayo was happy to share the recipe for her scones, which include a hint of orange and lemon zest. If you want, you can add dried fruit or nuts to make your own version. Mix the scones as you would a pastry crust, working the cold butter into the flour mixture.

3 eggs, divided
1¾ C. cream
½ tsp. vanilla
zest of ½ lemon
zest of ½ orange
2½ C. bread flour
2 C. cake flour
¾ C. plus 2 tbsp.
granulated sugar
5 tsp. baking powder
½ tsp. salt
1 C. (2 sticks) cold
butter, cubed
½ C. dried fruit or nuts,

1. Preheat oven to 375°F.

2. In a bowl, beat 2 eggs. Add the cream and vanilla and lemon and orange zest. Stir to combine. Set aside.

3. In a separate bowl, sift together bread and cake flours, sugar, baking powder and salt. Cut the butter into the mixture until it forms pea-size lumps. Add the reserved wet ingredients and dried fruit and gently stir until just incorporated.

3. Turn out onto a lightly floured work surface. With lightly floured hands, knead together slightly until the dry ingredients are blended. Press dough together at the edges and pat out to about 1-inch thickness, cut into desired shapes and transfer to parchment-lined baking sheets.

4. In a bowl, beat remaining egg and ½ teaspoon water. Brush over scones.

5. Bake for 10-15 minutes, or until golden brown. Remove from oven. Serve warm.

"We pride ourselves on using whole ingredients, and I think it's the fat factor that elevates a scone beyond a biscuit. That and the little bit of love we put into each one."
Dan Einstein

CASEY'S
DAWGS
HOT DOGS
WITH
STEAMED BUNS
CHIPS • SODAS
Bulldog
Country
CHILI SLAW
CHEESE KRAUT
BROWNIES COOKIES
BAR-B-Q • CHICKEN STEW

HELL'S HALF POUNDER

Casey's is a throwback. Located in a nondescript corner building about 45 minutes north of Atlanta, Casey's might be know for their dogs, but it can be argued that they have the best hamburger that this author has ever crossed his lips. Don't be thrown off by the name. It has spice, yes, but the sweet heat blending of flavours is a masterful mix guaranteed to please the most finicky of tastes.

Hell sauce:
½ c. apple juice
½ c. pineapple chunks
⅛ c. brown sugar
⅛ c. honey
3 jalapenos
1 habanero pepper

Seasoning:
¼ tsp onion powder
¼ tsp garlic powder
½ tsp salt
½ tsp fresh ground pepper
¼ tsp chipotle cayenne powder (substitute ⅛ tsp of cayenne with ⅛ tsp of smoked paprika if unable to find)

Burger:
⅓ lb. fresh ground chuck steak
1 bun (non-sesame)
1 slice white American cheese (available at a good deli)
1 slice yellow American cheese (not Kraft singles!)
Butter

1. Hand grind the two peppers for the Hell's sauce until completely pureed.
2. Blend all Hell's sauce together in a blender and set aside.

Seasoning:
1. Mix all ingredients together into a shaker

Burger:
1. Gently mix hamburger meat with 1 tsp of seasoning into a patty shape.
2. Dry toast the bun on a griddle, both sides.
3. Fry the burger on the griddle with just a dollop of salted butter.
4. Baste both sides with the Hell's sauce.
5. Add both cheese slices to the almost cooked burger and cover with a pot lid to steam for 15 seconds.
6. Assemble the burger, adding a generous spoon of Hell's sauce to the bottom.
7. Enjoy. And thank your lucky stars for Casey's.

"You can find your way across this country using burger joints the way a navigator uses stars..."
Charles Kuralt

Fresh Apple Pie

Chequers Seafood Grill is an upscale seafood restaurant in Dunwoody offering simply-prepared fresh fish, premium steaks, an impressive wine cellar and handcrafted cocktails. Our chic-casual atmosphere suits any occasion, with seamless service and imaginative seafood dishes that truly set us apart from other seafood restaurants in Atlanta.

Filling:
10 Granny Smith apples, peeled and cored
½ C. (1 stick) butter
½ C. bourbon
¾ C. granulated sugar
¼ C. dried cherries
¼ C. cinnamon-sugar

Topping:
¾ C. all-purpose flour
½ C. granulated sugar
½ C. light brown sugar
1½ tbsp. ground cinnamon
¼ tsp. salt
½ C. (1 stick) salted butter, cut into pieces, room temperature
1 C. walnut pcs., coarsely chopped
vanilla ice cream (optional)

For the Filling:

1. Preheat oven to 400°F.

2. Cut apples into quarters, then into ½-inch slices. Place apples on cookie sheets and bake for 5 minutes.

3. In a large skillet over medium-high heat, melt the butter. Add the apples and sauté for 2 minutes. Add the bourbon and cook for 30 seconds. Add the sugar, dried cherries and cinnamon-sugar.

4. Gently and quickly stir the apples until well-coated and cook for 2 minutes or until sauce thickens and is forming small bubbles.

5. Divide filling into 6 ramekins or casserole dishes with a 1¼ cup capacity.

For the Topping:

1. Lower oven temperature to 350°F.

2. In a bowl, whisk together flour, sugar, brown sugar, cinnamon and salt.

3. Add butter and gently blend in with fingertips to form a topping that is moist and crumbly, the size of small peas (if necessary, add additional butter 1 teaspoon at a time if too dry).

4. Mix in walnuts. Distribute topping over pies.

5. Bake for 10 minutes. Serve warm, topped with ice cream.

CHEQUERS SEAFOOD GRILL
236 PERIMETER CENTER PARKWAY

"Good apple pies are a considerable part of our domestic happiness."
Jane Austen

While most think of the wonderful selection of meats when they think of Chops, the restaurant offers outstanding vegetables. This Mushroom Gratin is certainly one of them. Chef Rickey Figueroa offers the gratin with or without the Asiago cheese topping.

Signature Taste of ATLANTA

1 tbsp. unsalted butter
¼ C. chopped shallots
1 lb. button mushrooms, quartered
¼ C. white wine
½ tbsp. salt and pepper (mixed)
1 C. heavy cream
2 tbsp. grated Asiago cheese

1. Preheat the broiler.

2. In a large skillet, melt the butter over medium heat. Add the shallots and sauté, stirring occasionally until softened, 3-5 minutes.

3. Add the mushrooms, wine and salt/pepper mix and cook until all the liquid evaporates.

4. Add cream and reduce to a sauce consistency. Taste for seasoning.

5. Transfer mixture to an ovenproof serving dish and top with Asiago cheese. Place under the broiler until the cheese melts.

70 W. Paces Ferry Road at Peachtree Road

CHOPS

"If only one could tell true love from false love as one can tell mushrooms from toadstools."
Katherine Mansfield

APPLE AND GREEN PAPAYA SALAD

Co'm Dunwoody is a family-owned and operated restaurant that incorporates what we call "Vietnamese-French Grill Fusion." It brings together the long history and variety of many Vietnamese cooking styles, from classic and traditional Vietnamese dishes to more elegant French-influenced meals. Our family has resided in the Atlanta area for more than 30 years, and we are proud to be a part of the Dunwoody Neighborhood. We operate Co'm Dunwoody with the same passion for fine food that our grandparents had. Our mission is to provide Atlanta with fine and elegant dishes that combine traditional Vietnamese flavors with the additional touch of French delight.

4 tsp. granulated sugar
2 tsp. rice vinegar
5 tbsp. water
2 oz. (1 small) carrot, julienned
2 oz. Chinese daikon, julienned
6 oz. green papaya, julienned
6 oz. green mango, julienned
4 oz. (1 small) Fuji apple, julienned
4 oz. cucumber, peeled, seeded, and julienned
10 mint leaves, cut into ribbons
10 basil leaves, cut into ribbons
6 sprigs cilantro, chopped
2 tbsp. chopped salted peanuts, divided
2 tbsp. fried shallots, divided
additional mint and basil leaves for garnish

Co'm Salad Dressing:
4 tbsp. fish sauce
½ C. water
2 tbsp. lime juice
2 small red chiles, seeded and chopped
2 cloves garlic, chopped
1 tbsp. fresh orange juice
1 tbsp. rice vinegar
1½ tsp. honey
2 tsp. granulated sugar
1 tbsp. coconut juice (not milk), optional

1. In a small glass bowl, combine sugar, vinegar and water. Add carrot and daikon and stir to coat. Allow to marinate overnight, stirring occasionally.

2. Lift the carrot and daikon out of the pickling liquid and place in a large serving bowl. Add the papaya, mango, apple, cucumber, mint, basil and cilantro and lightly toss. Add all but 2 tsp. of the chopped peanuts and 1 tbsp. of the fried shallots.

3. Toss with the dressing, then garnish with the reserved peanuts and fried shallots and additional chopped fresh mint and basil.

For Co'm Salad Dressing:
1. In a small bowl, combine fish sauce, water, lime juice, chiles, garlic, orange juice, rice vinegar, honey, sugar and coconut juice, if using.

CO'M DUNWOODY VIETNAMESE GRILL

4005-E BUFORD HIGHWAY

"We need a couple of winners out of here, such as papaya or coffee, to be able to subsidize the other projects. We're getting very close in that effort."
Michael Conway

Commune in Midtown West offers a formidable mixture of great architecture, a romantic post-industrial location and wine savvy. This sleek newcomer has been able to charm a diverse and sophisticated clientele. New chef Thomas Ricci has more panache and technique than his predecessor, and the contemporary American style he polished in San Francisco serves Atlanta well. The ahi tuna tartare with lime avocado is a riot of fun flavors.

⅓ C. pimentón picante (hot Hungarian paprika)
⅓ C. ground ginger
¼ C. Kosher salt
4 lbs. baby back ribs (about 4 slabs)
2 tbsp. vegetable oil
1½-2 yellow onions, finely diced
1½-2 jalapeño peppers, finely diced
½ habanero pepper, finely diced
1 C. brown sugar
1 C. dark molasses
½ C. lime juice
1 C. apple cider vinegar
½ gal. (2 qt.) Coca-Cola

1. Preheat a convection oven to 200°F or a standard oven to 250°F.

2. In a bowl, combine pimentón picante, ginger and salt. Rub evenly over ribs, just to cover, not to cake. Discard excess rub.

3. Place ribs in a shallow baking dish or on a baking sheet and bake for 4 hours, until tender. Set aside to cool.

4. An hour before ribs are ready: In a large pot heat oil over medium heat. Sauté onions, jalapeños and habanero until tender, about 5-10 minutes. Add sugar and cook until dissolved. Add molasses, lime juice and vinegar. Reduce by ⅓ over medium heat. Add Coke and reduce by half until thickened, but not syrupy, stirring occasionally.

5. When ribs have cooled, cut into individual ribs. Place ribs in the sauce and glaze to your liking, reducing further if desired. Bathe ribs generously in sauce and serve.

COMMUNE
1198 HOWELL MILL ROAD

"Without a Coca-Cola life is unthinkable."
Henry Miller

COWTIPPERS

STEAKS & SPIRITS

COCONUT CAKE

If any one word could sum up Cowtippers it would be "surprise." Established in 1993, Cowtippers was conceived as a casual steak house in a "honky tonk" atmosphere. The original brick walls and aged wood of the 60-year old building were accented with eclectic art and artifacts, while a Texas-sized patio was constructed around a giant river birch tree. Today, Cowtippers is home to traditional steak house fare served with surprisingly creative twists, in a surprisingly relaxed atmosphere with surprising value pricing.

Coconut Cake:
4 egg whites
½ C. (1 stick) butter
½ C. Crisco
2 C. granulated sugar
5 egg yolks
2 C. all-purpose flour
1 tsp. baking soda
1 C. buttermilk
½ tbsp. vanilla extract
¾ C. Coco Lopez Cream of Coconut

Cream Cheese Frosting:
¾ C. (1½ sticks) butter, cold
12 oz. cream cheese, cold
1½ tsp. vanilla extract
5 C. confectioners' sugar
1 C. sweetened, flaked coconut

For the Coconut Cake:
1. Preheat a convection oven to 300°F or conventional oven to 325°F. Coat two 9-inch baking pans with non-stick spray and set aside.
2. Beat egg whites until stiff and set aside.
3. With an electric mixer on medium-low speed, beat butter, Crisco, sugar and egg yolks for 4-5 minutes or until light and fluffy, scraping down the bottom and sides of the bowl periodically.
4. In a separate bowl, sift flour and baking soda. Alternate adding flour mixture and buttermilk to batter, starting and ending with flour. Scrape down sides and bottom of bowl. Add vanilla extract and fold in beaten egg whites.
5. Divide batter into pans. Bake for 35-45 minutes, or until a tester inserted in the cake comes out clean and tops are golden. Set on a rack to cool.
6. Carefully cut the cakes in half horizontally. Sprinkle Coco Lopez Cream of Coconut over the layers, letting it soak in. Set aside.

For the Frosting:
1. With an electric mixer, beat butter until smooth. Add cream cheese and continue beating until smooth. Add the vanilla extract. Gradually add the confectioners' sugar and beat until frosting is smooth and creamy.

To Assemble:
1. Place one cake layer on a serving plate and top with frosting, repeat with three other layers. Frost sides of cake, being careful not to get any crumbs in the frosting. Coat tops and sides of cake with coconut.

COWTIPPERS
1600 PIEDMONT AVE

"It isn't the flavor of coconut that troubles me, but the texture I feel as if I'm chewing on a sweetened cuticle."
Steve Almond

PEACH ICE CREAM PIE

There's something about this frozen dessert that's truly addictive. Maybe it's the way the partially cooked peaches taste tart and mellow at the same time. Or how the vanilla cookie crust stays crisp even as the ice cream softens on your plate. Or the way, as each forkful of ice cream melts in your mouth, the bits of peach remain icily al dente. Whatever it is, you'll have trouble putting the leftovers back in your freezer — you'll want to eat it all at once.

Signature Tastes of ATLANTA

1 C. granulated sugar, divided
½ tsp. ground cinnamon
1 tsp. vanilla extract
4 C. (about 4 whole) peeled and sliced peaches, divided
45 vanilla wafers, divided
¼ C. butter, melted
1½ qt. vanilla ice cream
1 C. heavy whipping cream

1. In a medium saucepan, combine ½ cup granulated sugar, cinnamon and vanilla extract.

2. Chop 2 cups of the peaches into small pcs. and stir them into the sugar mixture (reserve remaining 2 cups of peaches for the peach sauce, below). Cook the mixture over medium heat about 5 minutes, until the sugar is dissolved and the mixture is bubbly but the peaches are still crisp. Remove from heat and cool completely, about 1 hour.

For the Crust:

1. In the bowl of a food processor, combine 35 of the vanilla wafers and 2 tbsp. granulated sugar and process until fine. Add the melted butter and process until well-combined. Press the mixture into the bottom and up the sides of a 9-inch pie pan. Freeze the crust about 30 minutes.

2. Allow the vanilla ice cream to sit at room temperature until slightly softened, about 15 minutes. Coarsely crush the remaining 10 vanilla wafers. Place the ice cream in a large bowl and carefully stir in the cooled peach mixture and the coarsely crushed wafers until the ice cream is just swirled in a marble pattern. Pour the filling into the crust, mounding in the center and smoothing the surface, and freeze until hard, at least 3 hours.

For the Peach Sauce and Whipped Cream:

1. In a food processor or blender, combine the remaining 2 cups peaches with ¼ cup sugar. Puree and store the peach sauce in the refrigerator.

2. To prepare the sweetened whipping cream, beat the cream with the remaining 2 tbsp. sugar until soft peaks form. Store in the refrigerator.

To Serve:

1. Drizzle each dessert plate with peach sauce. Place a slice of pie on top of the sauce, then top the pie with whipped cream.

DAILEY'S DOWNSTAIRS
17 ANDREW YOUNG INTERNATIONAL BLVD.

"Age does not diminish the extreme disappointment of having a scoop of ice creamfall from the cone."
Jim Fiebig

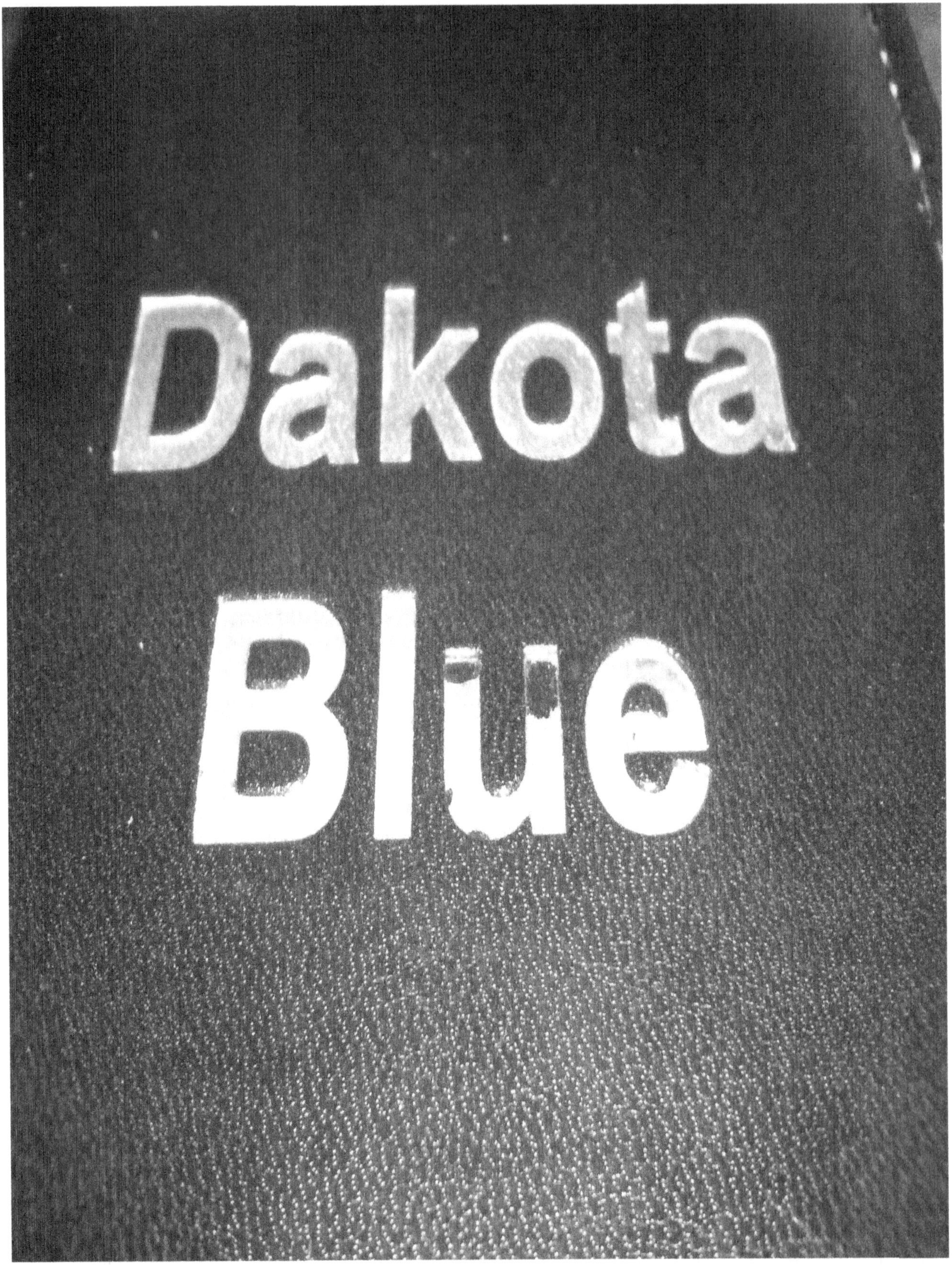
Dakota
Blue

Owner Alan Conner insists there's nothing particularly sexy about his veggie chili. "We're not a fancy restaurant; we're there for people's convenience," he said. And yet the chili has a loyal following. Conner's theory: "It's just hardy, spicy and super healthy."

2 poblano peppers
3 tbsp. canola oil
1 C. finely chopped onion (about 1 medium)
1 C. finely chopped celery (about 3 ribs)
1 C. finely chopped carrots (about 2 large)
1 tsp. salt
1 (12-oz.) package frozen meatless ground-beef substitute, such as Morningstar Farms brand
2 (28-oz.) cans crushed tomatoes
2 tbsp. ground cumin
2 tbsp. chili powder, or to taste
1½ tsp. ground cayenne, or to taste
1½ tsp. dried basil
1½ tsp. dried marjoram
1½ tsp. dried oregano
½ C. ketchup
½ C. balsamic vinegar
½ C. red wine
3 (16-oz.) cans pinto beans, rinsed and drained
1 (16-oz.) can black beans, rinsed and drained
hot sauce, such as Red Rooster brand, to taste
¼ C. finely chopped fresh cilantro

1. On a grill or directly over gas burner on the stovetop, roast the poblano peppers, turning them occasionally with tongs, until the skin is blackened and blistered. Place the peppers in a paper bag until they cool, about 5 to 10 minutes.

2. Meanwhile, in a large pot over medium heat, add the oil. Add the onion, celery, carrots and salt; cover and cook the vegetables for about 5 minutes, until soft.

3. When the poblanos are cool enough to handle, rub off the blackened skin under cold running water. Stem and seed the peppers, then dice. Add them to the cooking vegetables.

4. When the vegetables are soft, add the meatless crumbles, tomatoes, cumin, chili powder, cayenne, basil, marjoram, oregano, ketchup, vinegar, red wine, pinto beans and black beans.

5. Bring to a simmer, reduce the heat to low, partially cover the pot and simmer for 1 to 1 ½ hours, stirring occasionally. (If the chili seems too thick add water.)

6. Season to taste with hot sauce, additional salt and additional spices, if desired. Before serving, stir in the cilantro.

454 Cherokee Avenue Southeast

Dakota Blue

"An onion can make people cry but there's never been a vegetable that can make people laugh."
Will Rogers

SURF & TURF
DANTANNA'S
TURF
STEAKS
FRESH SEAFOOD
SALADS
PRIME RIB

Signature Taste of ATLANTA

Dantanna's combines culinary excellence with the entertainment value of sports to create the ultimate restaurant experience. With locations downtown and in Buckhead, we are Atlanta's only upscale sports restaurant that exudes the sophistication and elegance of a five-star restaurant and excitement and entertainment of having a private box at your favorite game.

Short Ribs:
6 lb. beef short ribs, about 6 (2x6-in.) pcs.
Kosher salt and ground black pepper
2 tbsp. canola oil
½ bottle dry red zinfandel or other dry red wine
4 C. reduced-sodium beef stock or broth
1 (12-oz.) package frozen blackberries, thawed & pureed, divided
2 C. coarsely chopped onions
1 C. coarsely chopped celery
1 C. coarsely chopped carrots
8 sprigs fresh thyme
6 bay leaves
5 garlic cloves
4 sprigs fresh rosemary
1 tbsp. black peppercorns

Sauce:
8 oz. bacon, preferably applewood-smoked, diced
½ C. diced onions
2 tbsp. minced garlic
2 C. ketchup
2 C. chile sauce
½ C. light brown sugar
¼ C. molasses
¼ C. Worcestershire sauce
1 tsp. Tabasco sauce
¼ C. lemon juice
salt and pepper

For the Ribs:
1. Preheat the oven to 350°F.
2. Dry ribs with a paper towel and season generously with salt and pepper.
3. In a large Dutch oven or ovenproof skillet heat oil over high heat. When hot, add ribs in batches and sear on all sides. Remove ribs and set aside. Discard excess oil from the pan.
4. Add wine, broth, 2 cups blackberry puree, onions, celery, carrots, thyme, bay leaves, garlic, rosemary and peppercorns and stir well to combine.
5. Return ribs to pan and bring to a simmer. Cover and transfer to oven. Braise for 3 hours.
6. When ribs are finished cooking, remove meat from pan and reserve.
7. Strain braising liquid, discarding all solids. Skim off excess fat. Place liquid in saucepan over medium-high heat and reduce by two-thirds while skimming and discarding all impurities as they come to the surface. Reserve liquid to add to the sauce (below).

For the Sauce:
1. In a large, heavy-bottomed skillet, cook bacon until crisp. Drain all but 2 tablespoons of fat.
2. Add onions and cook until translucent. Add garlic and stir to combine. Add ketchup, chile sauce, brown sugar, molasses, Worcestershire sauce, Tabasco, lemon juice and remaining blackberry puree.
3. Simmer on low heat for 45 minutes, stirring frequently to prevent sticking. Season with salt and pepper. Strain sauce and discard solids. Return to pan.
4. Add reduced braising liquid to sauce and warm through. Serve ribs with sauce.

DANTANNA S
3400 AROUND LENOX DRIVE

"If beef is your idea of real food for real people you'd better live real close to a real good hospital."
Neal Barnard

Signature Tastes of ATLANTA

You don't have to look past Dish's first menu item – rosemary pine nut popcorn – to know that chef and owner Sheri Davis is all about innovative food pairings. So it should come as no surprise that her version of fried calamari comes with a twist. The hot seafood is tossed in a bright lemon-honey dressing and surrounded by herbed mixed greens.

1 lb. calamari
1 C. milk
vegetable oil for frying
1 C. semolina flour
1 C. durum flour
¼ C. cornstarch
1 tbsp. salt
1½ tsp. white pepper
1½ tsp. onion powder
1½ tsp. garlic powder
⅔ C. Creamy Lemon Dressing (recipe below), divided
¼ C. chopped mixed fresh herbs, such as chives, basil, mint, Italian parsley and chervil, divided
8 C. loosely packed field greens

1. Clean the calamari in cold water and cut the tubes crosswise into ¼-inch rings.

2. Soak the calamari in the milk. Set aside.

3. In a fryer or deep pot, heat oil to 375°F. Combine the semolina, durum flour, cornstarch, salt, pepper and onion and garlic powders.

4. Dredge the calamari in the flour mixture, shake off excess and then place in the fryer. Fry until golden brown, about 3-5 minutes. Drain on paper towels.

5. Place the hot calamari in a bowl and toss with about ⅓ C. Creamy Lemon Dressing and about half the chopped fresh herbs.

6. Toss the field greens with the remaining herbs and dressing. Divide the greens among 4 plates. Surround the greens on each plate with ¼ of the hot calamari.

Creamy Lemon Dressing
1 egg yolk
2 tsp. red pepper flakes
1 tbsp. Dijon mustard
3 tbsp. rice wine vinegar
½ C. fresh lemon juice, divided
2 C. blended oil (75% canola and 25% olive)
¼ C. honey
salt, to taste

For the Creamy Lemon Dressing:
1. In a blender, combine the egg yolk, red pepper flakes, mustard, vinegar and about half the lemon juice.

2. With the motor running, slowly add the oil a few drops at a time, then increasing to a steady stream until dressing is emulsified.

3. Add additional lemon juice to taste.

4. Add honey to taste, to balance the tartness. Season with salt to taste.

870 N. HIGHLAND AVE. N.E.

DISH

"I believe that if life gives you lemons, you should make lemonade... And try to find somebody whose life has given them vodka, and have a party."
Ron White

Eggplant Salad with Pine Nuts and Sultanas

Executive chef Micah Willix said he serves his eggplant salad as a small "Taste and Share" item on Ecco's menu to tempt more people to try the exotic combination. "Having a small plate of something is not that big a commitment," he explained. "It's a great little salad that's different; you don't see it everywhere."

5 Japanese eggplants, cut into ½-in. half moons
2 shallots, chopped
3 tbsp. olive oil, divided
salt and pepper
¼ C. sultanas (golden raisins)
1 red bell pepper
¼ C. pine nuts
1 tsp. minced fresh rosemary
1 tsp. chopped fresh basil
2 tbsp. balsamic vinegar

1. Preheat oven to 375°F.

2. In a 9x13-inch roasting pan or baking dish, combine the eggplants and shallots with 1 tbsp. olive oil. Stir well to lightly coat all the eggplant. Season lightly with salt and pepper. Roast 20 to 30 minutes, until brown.

3. While eggplant is roasting, place the raisins in a small bowl and cover with hot water. Set aside.

4. On top of a gas burner or grill, roast the bell pepper directly over a flame, turning occasionally with tongs, until completely blackened, about 5 minutes. Transfer to a brown paper bag, seal and let steam about 10 minutes. When the pepper is cool enough to handle, rub under cool running water to remove blackened skin. Remove stem and seeds. Slice half the roasted pepper into ¼-inch strips. (Reserve remaining half for another use.)

5. In a small dry sauté pan, toast the pine nuts over medium heat, stirring occasionally to prevent burning, 2-3 minutes, until golden. Remove from heat and set aside.

6. In a large pan, heat remaining olive oil. Sauté the red pepper strips 1-2 minutes. Add the rosemary, basil, pine nuts and drained raisins. Saute 1-2 minutes, then add the roasted eggplant and shallots. Remove from heat, stir in the balsamic vinegar and season to taste with salt and pepper. Cool to room temperature before serving.

40 Seventh St. N.E.

Ecco

"I doubt that the imagination can be suppressed. If you truly eradicated it in a child, he would grow up to be aneggplant."
Ursula K Le Guin

BROWN BREAD ICE CREAM

Signature Tastes of ATLANTA

Fadó is an Irish term meaning 'long ago.' At Fadó we are telling the tale of Ireland's rich and celebrated Pub culture – a culture of hearty food and drink, good music, warm hospitality and friendly banter. In the tradition of Irish Pubs today and long ago, it's the Irish spirit that makes a Fadó. The original Atlanta Fadó opened in January 1996 at the corner of Peachtree Road and Buckhead Avenue and became an instant hit with the people of Atlanta.

1 C. whole wheat bread (approx. 3 slices)
¼ C. light brown sugar
3 tbsp. butter
8 egg yolks
2 C. sugar
1 tsp. cornstarch
2 tsp. pure vanilla extract (or 1 vanilla bean pod)
4 C. whole milk
2 C. heavy cream
1 tbsp. Grand Marnier (optional)

1. Preheat oven to 350ºF. Whiz the bread in the food processor to make breadcrumbs. Mix the brown sugar with the melted butter and add the breadcrumbs, stir well then spread the mixture on a baking sheet.
2. Bake the crumbs for 15-20 minutes, turning from time to time until they are toasted and crisp. Allow to cool. Break crumbs a bit into little nuggets. Store cooled crumbs in plastic bag until ready to use.
3. Cut the vanilla pod open and scrape out the seeds. Pour the milk into a heavy-based saucepan, add the vanilla pod and seeds and bring to a boil. Remove from the heat and leave for 15 minutes to allow the flavors to infuse. (Add vanilla extract to heated milk, if using.)
4. Whisk the egg yolks, sugar and cornstarch in a bowl until thick and pale. Gradually pour on the hot milk, whisking constantly. Return the mixture to the pan and cook over a gentle heat, stirring constantly. When the custard thickens and coats the back of the spoon, strain out the pod, add the Grand Marnier and chill in the refrigerator for 6-8 hours or overnight for best results.
5. When ready to make the ice cream, stir the cream into the chilled custard mixture and churn the mixture until thick but not solid. You need to "listen" to the churn, when it slows and strains then stop the motor to add the breadcrumbs. Rub the breadcrumbs between your fingers to break up any clumps. Stir the crumbs into the mixture, churn for another 10 minutes or until motor stops. Serve immediately or you can place in freezer and enjoy over several days.

FAD IRISH PUB
3035 PEACHTREE RD NE

"Good bread is the most fundamentally satisfying of all foods; and good bread with fresh butter, the greatest of feasts."
James Beard

Salmon with Spicy Thai Coconut Curry Sauce

At Five Seasons we believe fresh food and fresh beer taste better. Locally grown organic meats and vegetables are better for us, our guests, our community and the environment. A fresh, hand-crafted beer simply tastes better and brewing our own gives us the freedom to make many wonderful styles that change with the seasons.

Signature Tastes of ATLANTA

Five Seasons Brewing Co.
5600 Roswell Rd NE

Coconut Curry Sauce:
2 cans coconut milk, shaken well
½ C. heavy cream
½ C. fish or low-sodium chicken stock
2 tbsp. red curry paste
2 tbsp. tomato paste
1 tbsp. minced garlic
1 tbsp. minced shallot
1 tbsp. diced carrot
1 tbsp. diced celery
1 tbsp. diced onion
1½ tsp. fish sauce
1½ tsp. salt
½ C. fresh basil leaves
2 tbsp. fresh-squeezed lemon juice
2 tbsp. fresh-squeezed lime juice

Vegetables:
1 tbsp. butter
1 tbsp. chopped shallot
1 tbsp. minced garlic
½ C. sliced wild mushrooms
½ C. julienned carrots
½ C. sliced green beans
½ C. julienned red peppers
½ C. julienned sweet onions
½ C. sugar snap peas
½ C. julienned squash

For the Fish:
3 lb. salmon fillets
salt and white pepper
2 tbsp. canola oil

For the Coconut Curry Sauce:
1. In a large saucepan or stockpot, combine coconut milk, cream, stock, red curry paste, tomato paste, garlic, shallot, carrot, celery, onion, fish sauce and salt. Simmer for 15 minutes.
2. Add basil, lemon juice and lime juice and simmer for 5 minutes.
3. Puree with an immersion blender or cool and puree with blender. Pass through a strainer and return to pot.

For the Vegetables:
1. In a skillet, melt butter over medium heat.
2. Add shallot and garlic and sauté until softened. Add mixture to curry sauce. Add mushrooms, carrots, green beans, red peppers, sweet onions, sugar snap peas and squash to curry sauce and stir to combine.
3. Reheat until veggies are just cooked through.

To Prepare Fish:
1. Sprinkle salmon with salt and pepper. In a large skillet, heat oil over medium-high heat. Add salmon and pan fry until done.
2. Transfer to individual plates, top salmon with sauce and vegetables.

"The shark heart slows down in the cold, just as our own heart would, ... But ... where our heart would simply stop, the salmon shark's keeps on ticking."
Barbara Block

FLOATAWAY CAFE

- established 1998 -

LEMONCELLO COLLINS

Located in a renovated warehouse, Floataway Café transformed the space into a contemporary dining experience. Chefs/Owners Anne Quatrano and Clifford Harrison have created a local organic, produce-driven menu with French, Mediterranean and Italian influences that changes as frequently as the farmers unload their daily harvest. Pale blues are offset by creamy wood panels and natural lighting, while a courtyard area is transformed into a romantic outdoor café with the night sky forming a starry canopy.

2 oz. lemoncello
2 oz. fresh lemon juice
1 to 1½ oz. Thyme Simple Syrup (recipe follows)
½ oz. Stolichnaya or other premium vodka
1 splash sparkling water or soda water

Garnish:
1 sprig fresh lemon thyme
1 lemon slice, seeded

Thyme Simple Syrup:
1 C. water
1 C. granulated sugar
5 to 6 sprigs lemon or plain thyme

To Prepare the Thyme Simple Syrup:
1. In a saucepan, heat water, sugar and thyme until sugar dissolves.

2. Place simple syrup in a jar with the thyme to infuse the liquid, 1 or more days. Remove thyme sprig. Refrigerate remaining simple syrup for later use.

To Prepare the Lemoncello Collins:

1. In a shaker filled with ice, combine lemoncello, lemon juice, generous 1 ounce simple syrup and vodka.

2. Shake well and pour into a tall collins glass.

3. Taste for balance and add simple syrup, if desired. (Bartender tasting tip: place a straw into the drink, cover the straw with your finger, remove the straw from the drink and taste through the end of the straw).

4. Top with a splash of sparkling water.

5. Garnish with a sprig of thyme and lemon slice.

FLOATAWAY CAFE
1123 ZONOLITE ROAD N.E.

"When life gives you lemons. . . You might as well shove 'em where the sun don't shine, because you sure as hell aren't ever going to see any lemonade."
Rob Thurman

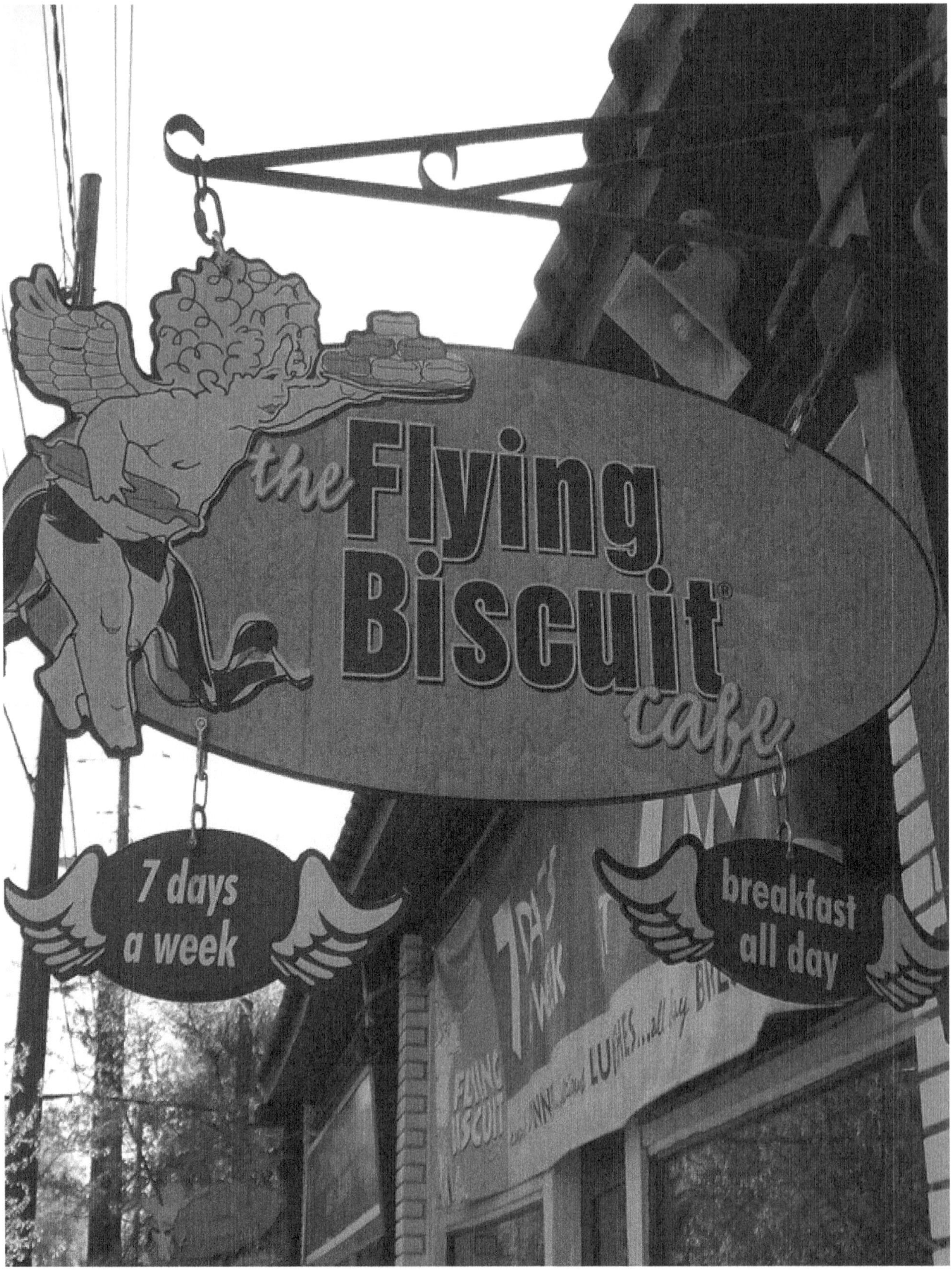
the Flying Biscuit® cafe
7 days a week
breakfast all day

CREAMY DREAMY WHITE CHEDDAR GRITS

Nestled among funky Craftsman bungalows in the heart of Historic Candler Park, the original location of The Flying Biscuit Cafe is one of Atlanta's favorite spots for brunch. Since we opened in 1993, the restaurant has tripled in size and the décor, like the food, is eclectic and cheerful. Be sure to visit the bakery right next door, so you can pick up biscuits for the road! The Flying Biscuit Cafe opens at 7 am and closes at 10 pm daily, serving non-stop all day.

6 C. water
2 C. half and half
1 tbsp. Kosher salt
¼ tsp. white pepper
2 C. quick grits
1 C. grated white cheddar cheese
4 tbsp. unsalted butter, cubed

1. In a saucepan, combine water, half and half, salt and white pepper and bring to a boil.

2. Slowly pour grits into boiling water while whisking the entire time. (Watch out for splattering; mixture is very hot.)

3. Reduce to low heat and continue to whisk often, until thick and completely smooth, about 10 minutes.

4. Add cheese and stir gently until cheese melts.

5. Whisk again to combine.

6. Turn heat off and allow grits to rest 5 minutes.

7. Add butter and stir until completely smooth, silky and shiny.

FLYING BISCUIT CAFE
1001 PIEDMONT AVE.

"Poets have been mysteriously silent on the subject of cheese."
G.K. Chesterton

The story of Fogo de Chão began in the mountainous countryside of Rio Grande do Sul in Southern Brazil, where its founders were born. Growing up, the brothers were immersed in the centuries-old Gaucho culture, a rich blend of traditions from European immigrants and Brazilian natives. An important element of this culture is churrasco, the Gaucho way of roasting meats over pits of open fire for delicious barbecues, which is always present at every festive occasion, especially family gatherings.

Black Beans:
½ lb. black beans
2 tbsp. vegetable oil
1 onion, minced
3 cloves of garlic, minced
4 slices bacon, cut in small pcs.
2 pork sausages, sliced
8 oz. pork loin, cut into small cubes
Tabasco, to taste
salt, to taste

Arroz Carreteiro (Old Wagon Rice):
2 C. white rice
1½ lb. charque (Brazilian beef jerky), cut in small cubes (optional)
1 tbsp. vegetable oil
1 onion, minced
1 tsp. minced garlic
2 tbsp. chopped parsley, (optional)
salt and pepper, to taste

For the Black Beans:

1. Soak the black beans in a bowl of water overnight.

2. Drain; cover with 1-inch of water in a large pot and bring to a boil. Skim off excess foam that forms on the surface.

3. In a skillet, add the oil and heat over medium heat. Sauté the onion until tender, about 5 minutes.

4. Add garlic and cook for 1 minute. Add to black beans and stir to combine. Reduce heat and simmer until tender, about 1 hour.

5. In a separate pan, cook the bacon, sausages and pork until cooked through. Add to beans and cook together for 10 minutes. Season with Tabasco and salt.

For the Arroz Carreteiro (Old Wagon Rice):

1. Cook the rice according to package directions.

2. In another pot, cover the charque with water and cook until very tender, 30-35 minutes.

3. In a large skillet, add oil and heat over medium heat. Cook onion, garlic and charque for 5 minutes. Add the rice and cook for 1 minute. Add parsley, salt and pepper.

"The budget is like a mythical bean bag. Congress votes mythical beans into it, then reaches in and tries to pull real ones out."
Will Rodgers

Arugula and Fresh Strawberries with Blue Cheese Vinaigrette

Serving hearty food with rural roots and an urban polish, Food 101 caters to those seeking a dining experience reminiscent of days gone by. Created by talented chef Justin Keith, the menu features proven classics with an inventive twist. This neighborhood Atlanta eatery exudes comfort not only through its food, but also through its relaxed atmosphere.

Signature Tastes of ATLANTA

Dressing:
¼ C. blue cheese
¼ C. red wine vinegar
¼ C. cider vinegar
1 C. canola oil
salt and pepper, to taste
Tabasco, to taste
½ tbsp. fresh parsley

Salad:
4 C. fresh cleaned arugula
12 large fresh sweet strawberries, sliced
1 C. blue cheese crumbles
¼ red onion, julienned

For the Dressing:

1. In a blender or food processor, pulse the blue cheese and the red wine and cider vinegars together to combine.

2. With the motor running, slowly add the oil in a small stream until the dressing emulsifies.

3. Transfer to a bowl and season with salt, pepper and Tabasco. Whisk in the parsley.

For the Salad:

1. In a serving bowl, toss the arugula with ⅓ dressing, or until lightly coated.

2. Top with strawberries, blue cheese crumbles and red onions.

1397 N Highland Avenue Northeast

Food 101

"Like the strawberry wives, that laid two or three great strawberries at the mouth of their pot, and all the rest were little ones."
Francis Bacon

PUREE OF WHITE BEAN SOUP

This restaurant is located in the heart of Atlanta, and you have to pay for parking. Additionally, the servers and other staff members are very attentive. Although, my waiter told me he doesn't read English, he knew the menu items well because he was French. I thought it was kind of funny when he said he couldn't read English because I didn't expect that.

3 C. dried white beans
2 tbsp. unsalted butter
4 oz. (4 slices) bacon, diced
1 large onion, chopped
1 leek (white part only), chopped
1 carrot, peeled and chopped
2 ribs celery, chopped
8 garlic cloves, chopped
10 C. low-sodium chicken broth
1 tbsp. fresh thyme
1 tsp. fresh rosemary
1 C. heavy cream
salt and white pepper, to taste
10 tsp. white truffle oil, or to taste

1. In a large bowl, cover beans with 2-inches of water and soak overnight. Drain and set aside.

2. In a large stockpot over medium heat, melt butter. Add bacon and cook just until it renders its fat.

3. Add the onion, leek, carrot, celery and garlic and sauté until tender, about 15 minutes.

4. Add the beans, chicken broth, thyme and rosemary and bring to a boil.

5. Cook over medium heat until beans are very tender, 1½ to 2 hours.

6. Add the cream and bring to a boil. Puree with an immersion blender or transfer to a blender or food processor to puree.

7. Season with salt and white pepper to taste. Ladle into individual bowls and garnish each serving with a drizzle of truffle oil.

FRENCH AMERICAN BRASSERIE
30 IVAN ALLEN JR. BLVD., SUITE 125

"A soup like this is not the work of one man. It is the result of a constantly refined tradition. There are nearly a thousand years of history in this soup."
Willa Cather

Fritti serves authentic Neopolitan Pizza as certified by the Verace Pizza Napoletana Association. Our pizza is prepared according to traditional artisanal methods. The dough is made with 00 Caputo flour, natural yeast, and sea salt. It is baked in a 1000°F wood burning oven, served Italian style whole, not sliced. Buon Appetito.

canola oil for frying
¾ C. water
¼ C. white wine
1 C. rice flour
2 tsp. finely chopped fresh rosemary
salt and pepper, to taste
2 lb. assorted wild mushrooms, such as crimini, shiitake and oyster, cleaned and cut into bite-size pcs.
truffle oil

1. Heat 2-inches of oil in a fryer or deep pot to 350°F.

2. Combine the water and wine, and then slowly whisk the liquid into the rice flour until the batter is the consistency of thick gravy.

3. Whisk in the rosemary and season the batter with salt and pepper.

4. Place the mushroom pieces in a large bowl. Add the batter mix to the mushrooms and toss until the mushrooms are lightly and evenly coated.

5. Fry the mushrooms in the oil until they are brown and crisp, about 3-4 minutes.

6. Drain the mushrooms on a paper towel, then drizzle very lightly with truffle oil and season with salt and pepper.

309 North Highland Ave.

FRITTI

"It is easy to love the people far away. It is not always easy to love those close to us. It is easier to give a cup of rice to relieve hunger than to relieve the loneliness and pain of someone unloved in our own home. Bring love into your home for this is where our love for each other must start."
Mother Teresa

CREAM OF MUSHROOM SOUP

The Gallery Cafe is located in Buckhead at the corner of Roswell and Piedmont road, in the Tuxedo shopping center. At "The Gallery," enjoy your meal while surrounded by a continually changing exhibition of original paintings from local artists. The Gallery Cafe features a large variety of all-fresh and homemade daily soups, salads, sandwiches and dressings. Try "Michele's Homemade Tarts."

**1 medium onion, chopped
3 large garlic cloves, finely minced
1 small celery rib, trimmed and chopped
5-6 large portobello mushrooms, chopped
3½ to 4 C. half and half or heavy cream
salt and freshly ground pepper
1 tbsp. chopped fresh parsley
truffle oil (optional)**

1. In a large saucepan over medium-high heat, add the oil.

2. Sauté the onion and garlic for 2-3 minutes, or until they begin to soften.

3. Add the celery and mushrooms and stir well to combine. Cook for 1 minute.

4. Add 3 ½ cups of half and half, salt and pepper to taste, and bring to a boil. Reduce the heat to medium-low, cover and simmer for 12 minutes.

5. Transfer the soup to a food processor or blender or use an immersion blender and process to obtain a smooth texture. If too thick, return to heat and add more half and half to thin.

6. Garnish with a pinch of parsley and 2 drops of truffle oil before serving.

3655 ROSWELL ROAD, SUITE 108

GALLERY CAFE

"Falling in love is like eating mushrooms, you never know if it's the real thing until it's too late."
Bill Balance

BLUE CHEESE RISOTTO

Garrison's Broiler and Tap pairs this tangy, creamy risotto with its grilled flat iron steak. "Blue cheese and steak go together naturally, and it's a marriage made in heaven," said Chef Craig LaPonzina. "The steak doesn't need anything; the risotto is enough flavor for it." LaPonzina had this advice for preparing risotto: "Keep stirring. Italians say if you make risotto right, you don't need to add any salt because the sweat from your brow is enough."

6 C. low-sodium chicken stock
2-3 slices bacon (2 oz.), diced
1 tbsp. butter
¼ C. diced yellow onion
1 C. Arborio rice
¼ C. white wine
¾ C. (4 oz.) crumbled blue cheese
white pepper, to taste

1. Pour chicken stock into a saucepan and heat over low. Do not boil. In a large saucepan over medium heat, cook the bacon until gently browned. Remove bacon and set aside.

2. Add butter and onion to bacon drippings in pan and cook, stirring, until onion is translucent, about 1 minute. Add rice and continue cooking and stirring for 2 more minutes. Add white wine to deglaze pan. Add enough warm chicken stock to cover rice completely.

3. Cook, stirring constantly, until most of liquid is absorbed.

4. Repeat this process, adding just enough liquid each time to cover the rice, until it is creamy and tender but still has just a hint of resistance when you bite into it— about 30 minutes. You will use most or all of the chicken stock.

5. Remove from heat. Stir in reserved bacon and the blue cheese until cheese is melted. Season with white pepper.

6. Allow risotto to sit 10 minutes before serving. It will thicken as it cools.

GARRISON'S BROILER AND TAP

4400 ASHFORD DUNWOODY ROAD

"Blue cheese contains natural amphetamines. Why are students not informed about this?"
Mark E. Smith

LOBSTER ENCHILADAS

Drawing inspiration from the famous Southwestern painter, Georgia O'Keeffe, the Georgia Grille intermingles the flavors of the Southwest with the hospitality of the South. For over 17 years, Karen Hilliard and her staff have been serving her unique interpretation of Southwestern fare in a casual, kicked-back style.

1½ tsp. oil
2 tbsp. diced shallot,
about 1 large
1 tbsp. pureed (mashed)
garlic, about 2 cloves
1 tbsp. pickled jalapeño
puree (see Note)
3 C. chicken stock
2 C. heavy cream
1 lb. cooked lobster
meat, cut into large dice
2¼ C. grated Monterey
Jack cheese (about 8 oz.),
divided
1 red bell pepper,
smoked, seeded, and
diced (see Note)
1 large tomato, diced
1 tbsp. minced cilantro
2 tsp. fresh lime juice
¼ tsp. marjoram
12 (8-in.) flour tortillas,
softened
1 C. fresh tomato salsa

1. In a large, heavy skillet over medium-high heat, heat the oil until hot. Add the shallots, garlic and jalapeño puree. Cook briefly, stirring constantly, until softened, 2-3 minutes. Add chicken stock and cook until reduced by half. Add the cream and continue cooking until reduced by half, stirring occasionally.

2. Stir in lobster, 1½ cups cheese, smoked bell pepper, tomato, cilantro, lime juice and marjoram. Do not boil or the mixture will separate. Set aside to keep warm.

3. Preheat broiler. Spoon about ¼ cup filling into each softened tortilla. Roll into a cylinder, and place the filled tortillas seam side down in an ovenproof casserole. Pour remaining sauce over the enchiladas. Sprinkle with the remaining cheese.

4. Place the casserole in the oven and broil just until cheese melts, about 2-3 minutes. Serve topped with fresh tomato salsa.

Note: The flavor of smoked red bell pepper in the sauce is a signature at Georgia Grille, where Hilliard says several are smoked at once in a large commercial smoker with hickory. You can create a similar taste at home with a stovetop smoker, which will take about 15 minutes; or on a grill or outdoor smoker, using hickory. An alternative is to omit the jalapeño puree and the smoked pepper and substitute about ½ chipotle pepper in adobo sauce, pureed.

GEORGIA GRILLE
2290 PEACHTREE ROAD

"Their steaks are often good, but the lobsters, with claws the size of Arnold Schwarzenegger's forearms, are as glazed and tough as most of the customers."
Malcolm S. Forbes

Signature Tastes of ATLANTA

Goldfish located off of Ashford Dunwoody Road in front of Perimeter Mall opened in the summer of 2000. The menu is a combination of pristine seafood, sushi and steaks. They feature the freshest fish from around the world. The interior boasts huge ceiling height and a massive oversized mural from Leigh Smith Catherall. There is a 600-gallon salt water aquarium with beautiful sea creatures. Live entertainment nightly makes Goldfish one of Atlanta's favorite places to meet for a fabulous cocktail and enjoy a first class dining experience!

Marinara Sauce:
3 lb. organic vine-ripe tomatoes
1 tbsp. grapeseed or olive oil
3 tbsp. chopped garlic
3 tbsp. chopped shallots
1 (14½-oz.) can high quality, whole peeled plum tomatoes, roughly chopped
salt and freshly ground black pepper
¼ C. chopped Italian parsley
¼ C. chopped basil

Grits:
2 C. half and half
2 C. heavy cream
scant 1 C. stone ground grits
½ tsp. chopped garlic
1 tsp. salt
4 oz. Monterey Jack cheese, shredded

Shrimp and Sausage:
1 tbsp. grapeseed or olive oil
1 lb. peeled and deveined large shrimp
salt and pepper
1¼ C. smoked andouille sausage, cut in half lengthwise and sliced

Garnish (optional):
5 tsp. basil oil
2 tbsp. chopped chives

For the Marinara Sauce:

1. Blanch the tomatoes in boiling water for 10-15 seconds. Remove skin and seeds and roughly chop. Set aside.

2. In a large sauté pot, add oil and heat over medium heat. Sauté garlic and shallots until translucent. Add reserved fresh tomatoes and canned tomatoes. Bring to a simmer and cook for 30 minutes over low heat. Remove from heat and season with salt and pepper. Add parsley and basil and stir to combine.

3. While the marinara sauce is simmering, prepare the grits. In a large pot, combine half and half and cream and bring to a boil (watch carefully to make sure it doesn't overboil). Add grits, garlic and salt. Reduce heat and slowly cook, stirring frequently, scraping the bottom of the pan, until grits liquid is absorbed and grits are cooked and tender, about 45 minutes. Add cheese and stir until combined.

To Make the Shrimp and Sausage:

1. In a sauté pan over medium-high heat, add oil. Add shrimp and cook until translucent. Season with salt and pepper. Reduce heat to medium, add sausage and cook for 1 minute. Add marinara sauce and cook for 3 minutes.

2. On individual bowls or plates, place ½ cup grits. Divide shrimp and marinara between plates and place beside grits. Drizzle basil oil on shrimp and top with chopped chives.

4400 ASHFORD DUNWOODY RD

GOLDFISH

"Shrimp is the fruit of the sea. You can barbecue it, boil it, broil it, bake it, sautée it. There's ... shrimp kebabs, shrimp creole, shrimp gumbo, pan fried, deep fried, stir fried. There's pineapple shrimp and lemon shrimp, coconut shrimp, pepper shrimp, shrimp soup, shrimp stew, shrimp salad, shrimp and potatoes, shrimp burger, shrimp sandwich ... That's about it."
Mykelti Williamson

Sun-Dried Tomato Caesar Salad

Young or old, single or married, with children or empty-nesters, Harvest is a place where all can come together and celebrate the land. Whether you want to purchase produce from our 12-acre working farm; visit one of our restaurants; buy hand-picked flowers or fresh honey from our open air farmers' market; or live in one of our homes, townhomes or flats, we have something for everyone.

½ C. sun-dried tomatoes
1 C. hot water
2 tbsp. Dijon mustard
¼ C. lemon juice
2 tbsp. roasted garlic paste
3 tbsp. freshly grated parmesan cheese
2 tsp. Worcestershire sauce
¼ tsp. minced garlic
1¼ C. olive oil
salt and white pepper
1 large head romaine lettuce

1. In a bowl, combine tomatoes and hot water and set aside.

2. In a bowl or food processor, combine mustard, lemon juice, roasted garlic paste, cheese, Worcestershire sauce and minced garlic. Pulse until combined. Slowly add olive oil until an emulsion forms. Season with salt and pepper.

3. When tomatoes have softened, remove from water, reserving water, and puree. If necessary, add a little reserved water until they form a smooth paste. Fold tomato puree into dressing.

4. In a bowl, mix lettuce with just enough dressing to lightly coat. Divide lettuce on four serving plates.

Harvest
853 N. Highland Ave.

"They eat the dainty food of famous chefs with the same pleasure with which they devour gross peasant dishes, mostly composed of garlic and tomatoes, or fisherman's octopus and shrimps, fried in heavily scented olive oil on a little deserted beach."
Luigi Barzini

Signature Tastes of ATLANTA

Thinly sliced mushrooms topped with greens make a perfect starter. Michael Arnett, general manager of Haven, was glad to supply the recipe. In addition to portobellos, the restaurant uses crimini, button and shiitake mushrooms. You can substitute your favorites or, to save time, use two (4-ounce) packages of sliced wild mushrooms, available at many supermarkets. The mushrooms are topped with a grated cheese, a dash of truffle oil, freshly cracked fleur de sel and a garnish of baby lettuce. Toss lettuce with your favorite vinaigrette or combine 2 teaspoons olive oil with 1 teaspoon champagne vinegar.

4 portobello mushrooms, peeled and gills cleaned
1 tbsp. plus 1 tsp. extra-virgin olive oil, divided
4 thyme sprigs
1 tsp. chopped garlic
salt and freshly ground pepper
1 tsp. butter
10 crimini mushrooms, sliced ⅛-in. thick
10 button mushrooms, sliced ⅛-in. thick
10 shiitake mushrooms, sliced ⅛-in. thick
2 shallots, finely chopped, divided
⅓ C. freshly grated Pecorino-Romano or Parmigiano-Reggiano cheese
fleur de sel or other sea salt
1 tbsp. truffle oil
1 C. assorted baby lettuces
2 tsp. champagne vinaigrette

1. Preheat oven to 325°F.

2. Place portobellos on a baking sheet and brush with 1 tablespoon olive oil. Top with thyme and garlic and sprinkle with salt and pepper.

3. Bake for 20-25 minutes, or until softened. Cool, discard thyme and slice mushrooms thinly on a diagonal. Set aside.

4. Meanwhile, in a skillet over medium heat, add butter and remaining teaspoon of olive oil.

5. Sauté crimini, button and shiitake mushrooms for 5-6 minutes, or until softened. Add half the shallots and season with salt and pepper. Stir to combine and cook 1 minute. Set aside to cool.

6. Arrange mushrooms on individual serving plates. Sprinkle with cheese, remaining shallots, freshly ground pepper and fleur de sel. Drizzle with truffle oil.

7. In a small bowl, toss baby lettuces with vinaigrette. Add as a garnish in the center of the mushrooms.

1441 Dresden Drive.

HAVEN

I am... a mushroom; On whom the dew of heaven drops now and then."
John Ford

Signature Tastes of ATLANTA

Henri's Bakery is known internationally and has won many awards for its creations. Henri's offers a wide range of scratch baked goods from bread and rolls to croissants, pastries, cookies, cakes, French pastries, pies, Danish, donuts, etc…as well as our signature deli sandwiches.

Shortbread Cookies:
1 C. granulated sugar
¾ C. (1½ sticks)
unsalted butter
1 C. vegetable shortening
6 egg yolks
4 C. cake flour
2 tsp. salt
2 tsp. vanilla extract

Fondant Filling:
½ C. granulated sugar
¼ C. water
2 tbsp. light corn syrup
2 C. powdered sugar
food coloring (optional)

For the Shortbread Cookies:
1. With an electric mixer on low speed, cream sugar with butter and shortening until thoroughly combined.
2. Slowly add egg yolks. Scrape the bowl and add flour, salt and vanilla.
3. Scrape bowl again to make sure ingredients are thoroughly mixed. Wrap dough in plastic and chill for several hours.
4. Preheat oven to 350°F. Roll out the dough a little at a time into log shapes the thickness of a roll of quarters. (Keep the remainder refrigerated.) Cut off pieces about 1½-inches in length.
5. Place pieces cut side up on a cookie sheet lined with parchment paper. Flatten each piece and make a depression in the middle using your finger or a dowel.
6. Bake for 15 minutes or until slightly brown around edges. Cool completely on rack.

Prepare Fondant Filling.
1. Boil sugar and water until dissolved.
2. Transfer to the bowl of an electric mixer and add corn syrup and powdered sugar.
3. Mix on low speed until smooth. Fondant should be thick yet pourable.
4. Correct the consistency with more powdered sugar or corn syrup if necessary. Tint with color if desired.
5. Using a small spoon or decorating bag, place fondant in center of each cookie. Fondant will harden upon standing.

HENRI'S BAKERY
6 IRBY AVE.

"Number one, I absolutely love making chocolate chip cookies. I mean, it's fun. It's exciting. Beyond the fact that I love making them, I love eating them.
Debbi Fields

SWEET POTATO PANCAKES

Stacey Eames was on a weekend getaway in the mountains when she and a friend happened upon a little diner. Breakfast was looking pretty dismal until Eames spotted the sweet potato pancakes on the menu. "They were delicious, so we added them to our menu," she said. Her recipe has been tweaked over time, but now Eames believes she has achieved "the ultimate in comfort food. Order them with a side of eggs, turkey sausage, bacon or ham for a perfect carbo-load/protein buzz."

Signature Tastes of ATLANTA

Pancakes:
2 medium-small sweet potatoes
¾ C. whole-wheat flour
¾ C. all-purpose flour
1 tbsp. baking powder
1 tsp. salt
½ tsp. nutmeg
¼ C. (½ stick) unsalted butter
2 eggs
1½ tbsp. packed brown sugar
1½ C. milk
vegetable oil for cooking
Brown Sugar Butter Sauce (see recipe)
toasted pecans for garnish

Brown Sugar Butter Sauce:
½ C.(1 stick) unsalted butter
1 C. packed brown sugar
¼ C. water

1. Scrub the sweet potatoes and pierce all over with a fork. Microwave 6 to 7 minutes on high, until they are easily pierced through with a knife or fork. Slit the sweet potatoes lengthwise and let cool enough so you can handle them, about 5 minutes.

2. Meanwhile, measure and sift together into a large mixing bowl the whole-wheat flour, all-purpose flour, baking powder, salt and nutmeg. Set aside.

3. When potatoes are still warm but not too hot to handle, spoon the flesh into a measuring cup When you have 1¼ cups, transfer to the bowl of a food processor. Add the butter and process until smooth. Add the eggs and brown sugar and blend until smooth. Add as much of the milk as the bowl can easily contain and blend.

4. Spoon the sweet potato mixture and remaining milk into the bowl with the dry ingredients. Mix with a spoon until just combined.

5. Heat a skillet or griddle lightly coated with vegetable oil on medium heat. Drop heaping spoonfuls of batter onto the hot griddle. When pancakes start to bubble, flip and cook until golden. Serve with Brown Sugar Butter Sauce and toasted pecans.

For Brown Sugar Butter Sauce:
1. In a medium saucepan over medium heat, melt the butter. Add the sugar and stir until sugar is dissolved. Whisk in the water and let simmer for 8 to 10 minutes.

HIGHLAND BAKERY
655 HIGHLAND AVE., NO. 10

"Love is a bicycle with two pancakes for wheels. You may see love as more of an exercise in hard work, but I see it as more of a breakfast on the go."
Jarod Kintz

HOLEMAN
AND FINCH
PUBLIC HOUSE

SHRIMP AND SMOKED OYSTER CHOWDER

Holeman and Finch Public House is just that, a public house. The arrangement of the tables and the seating in the establishment encourages conversation and communion – a sense that this is a community gathering. The menu is set up the same way. A meal here might be one or two items for one person or several items served up to share with companions or your neighbor seated at the bar.

3 C. water
1 C. bottled clam broth
½ lb. medium shrimp, shelled, deveined and quartered, shells reserved
6 garlic cloves; 4 smashed, 2 minced
¼ C. dry sherry
½ tsp. crushed red pepper
2 bay leaves
1 onion, chopped (about 1½ C.)
1 tbsp. extra virgin olive oil
1 small fennel bulb, cored and finely diced (½ C.)
1 celery rib, finely diced
1 small green bell pepper, finely diced
1 (14-oz.) can peeled Italian tomatoes, finely chopped and juices reserved
1 medium baking potato, peeled and cut into ½-inch pcs.
salt and freshly ground black pepper
6 oz. skinless grouper or cod fillet, cut into 1-in. pcs.
1 (3-oz.) can smoked oysters, drained and chopped
1 tbsp. Worcestershire sauce
1 C. buttermilk, at room temperature
2 tbsp. chopped flat-leaf parsley

1. In a large saucepan, combine the water and clam broth with the shrimp shells, smashed garlic, sherry, crushed red pepper, bay leaves and one third of the onion. Bring to a boil and simmer, covered, over low heat for 20 minutes. Strain the shrimp stock into a heat-proof bowl and discard the solids.

2. In a soup pot, heat the oil over medium heat. Add the fennel, celery, bell pepper, minced garlic and the remaining onion. Cover and cook over moderate heat, stirring once or twice, until the vegetables are barely softened, 3 minutes. Uncover and cook until tender, 3 minutes longer.

3. Add the tomatoes with their juices and the shrimp stock; bring to a simmer. Add the potato, season with salt and pepper and simmer until just tender, 15 minutes.

4. Add the shrimp, grouper, oysters and Worcestershire sauce; simmer until cooked through, 3 minutes.

5. Off the heat, stir in the buttermilk and parsley. Serve in deep bowls.

"The man who doesn't like oysters, the woman who cannot abide sardines. We know the type."
Harold Nicolson

CREAM CHEESE BROWNIES

Neesha and Beena Nana bake a different kind of cake every day at this cheery little cafe owned by their father, Chhotu Nana, who came to Atlanta via Zimbabwe and India. While the double chocolate, strawberry, lemon and other cakes are served only one day a week, the Cream Cheese Brownies are so acclaimed that they have earned a permanent place on the menu.

Cream Cheese Layer:
1 large egg
⅓ C. granulated sugar
5⅓ tbsp. butter, melted
⅓ C. self-rising flour
8 oz. cream cheese, softened
1 tsp. almond extract

Chocolate Layer:
½ C. (1 stick) butter, divided
2½ C. semisweet chocolate morsels
2 large eggs
⅓ C. granulated sugar
¾ C. plus 1 tbsp. packed brown sugar
⅔ C. self-rising flour
1 tsp. vanilla extract

1. Grease bottom of a 13x9-inch baking pan and set aside. Preheat oven to 350°F.

2. For the cream cheese layer: In a mixing bowl, combine egg, sugar and 5⅓ tbsp. melted butter. Stir in flour, cream cheese and almond extract. Spread evenly in prepared pan.

3. For the chocolate layer: In a small saucepan over low heat, melt 1 stick butter. Cool slightly. Pour 5½ tbsp. melted butter into a mixing bowl and leave remaining 2½ tbsp. in saucepan. Add chocolate morsels to saucepan and return to low heat, stirring constantly, until chocolate melts.

4. In the bowl containing melted butter, add the eggs and granulated and brown sugars. Stir in flour and vanilla. Pour in melted chocolate/butter mixture and combine well. Spread evenly on top of cream cheese layer. Drag a knife through the pan to swirl batters.

5. Place in oven and bake 35-40 minutes or until brownies test done. Cool on wire rack before cutting into bars.

HOMESPUN CAFE
2020 HOWELL MILL ROAD N.W.

"A little chocolate is like a love affair—an occasional sweet release that lightens the spirit. A lot of chocolate is like marriage—it seems so good at first but before you know it you've got chunky hips and a waddle-walk."
Linda Solegato

WILD RICE AND MUSHROOM SOUP

At Houston's on Peachtree Road, not only do we work closely with local farmers and purveyors to ensure the produce, meat, fish, and chicken are of the highest standard, but we also have our own personal herb garden to guarantee the freshest greens around. Relax in one of our intimate booths or enjoy patio dining while listening to a live jazz trio nightly. We look forward to welcoming you soon!

2 C. wild rice 4 tbsp. (½ stick) butter ½ lb. carrots, diced fine ¼ lb. leeks, diced fine 1 lb. sliced mushrooms ½ C. all-purpose flour ½ C. sherry 3 qt. vegetable stock 1 qt. heavy cream 2 tbsp. chopped fresh thyme 3 tbsp. chopped fresh parsley salt and pepper, to taste	**1.** Cook rice in 2 quarts water until just bloomed, about 40 minutes. **2.** In a large Dutch oven over medium-high heat, melt butter and add carrots and leeks. Cook, stirring constantly, for about 10 minutes. **3.** Add mushrooms and cook until soft; add flour and stir well. **4.** Deglaze pan with sherry and cook until slightly reduced. **5.** Add stock and stir well. Reduce heat to medium and cook for about 30 minutes. **6.** Add wild rice and heavy cream and continue cooking until heated through. **7.** Stir in thyme and parsley and season with salt and pepper.

2166 PEACHTREE ROAD NORTHWEST

HOUSTON'S

"Where life is colorful and varied, religion can be austere or unimportant. Where life is appallingly monotonous, religion must be emotional, dramatic and intense. Without the curry, boiled rice can be very dull."
C. Northcote Parkinson

Walnut Shrimp

Raymond Hsu, owner of both restaurants, graciously shared the recipe for this popular dish. Deep-fried shrimp and honeyed walnuts are coated with a sweetened mayonnaise-based dressing. There are several steps going on at once, although none is very time-consuming

¼ C., plus 1 tsp. honey, divided
1 tbsp. granulated sugar
1 tbsp. water
8 walnuts, toasted
canola or vegetable oil for frying
8-10 oz. peeled and deveined large shrimp
1 egg, beaten
½ C. cornstarch
3 tbsp. mayonnaise
½ tsp. lemon juice
1 tsp. sweetened condensed milk

1. In a saucepan, heat ¼ cup honey, sugar and water until sugar dissolves. Coat walnuts with sauce, letting excess drip off, and set them on wax paper to dry.

2. Heat about 2-inches of oil in a deep fryer or saucepan to 325 to 350 degrees.

3. Dip shrimp in egg and coat with cornstarch. Fry shrimp in batches until golden brown. Transfer to paper towels to drain.

4. Meanwhile, in a double boiler or bowl over simmering water, combine mayonnaise, 1 teaspoon honey, lemon juice and condensed milk. Heat just until warm. Add shrimp and walnuts and toss to coat. Serve immediately.

HSU'S GOURMET
192 PEACHTREE CENTER AVE.

"Shrimp is the fruit of the sea. You can barbecue it, boil it, broil it, bake it, sautée it. There's ... shrimp kebabs, shrimp creole, shrimp gumbo, pan fried, deep fried, stir fried. There's pineapple shrimp and lemon shrimp, coconut shrimp, pepper shrimp, shrimp soup, shrimp stew, shrimp salad, shrimp and potatoes, shrimp burger, shrimp sandwich... That's about it."
Mykelti Williamson

GINGERBREAD PUDDING WITH MEYER LEMON CURD

Atlanta's new neighborhood cool spot, JCT. Bar, evokes a welcoming, low-key rooftop environment perfect for relaxing or entertaining friends. An extensive selection of cool refreshers, a delicious small Southern plates menu, enjoyable live music and comfortable lounge areas make JCT. Bar the place to be!

Gingerbread:
1 egg
¾ C. granulated sugar
½ C. sour cream
¼ C. plus 2 tbsp. water
1½ tbsp. orange juice
1 C. molasses
¾ C. (1½ sticks) butter, melted
2 C. all-purpose flour
1⅛ tsp. baking soda
1½ tsp. ground ginger
1½ tsp. ground cinnamon
½ tsp. ground cardamom
¾ tsp. ground cloves
¾ tsp. ground nutmeg
¾ tsp. ground white pepper

Bread Pudding Soak:
2 C. heavy cream
2 C. half and half
⅓ C. granulated sugar
½ vanilla bean
6 egg yolks

Meyer Lemon Curd:
1 C. granulated sugar
zest of ½ lemon
¼ C. plus 2 tbsp. Meyer lemon juice* (about 2 lemons)
1 egg plus 1 yolk
1½ C. (3 sticks) unsalted butter, room temperature

If Meyer lemons are unavailable, the recipe works equally well with regular lemons

For the Gingerbread:
1. Preheat oven to 350°F. Grease and flour a 9x13-inch cake pan.
2. In a mixing bowl, preferably with a whisk attachment, whip the egg and sugar until light and fluffy. Add sour cream, water and orange juice.
3. In a separate bowl, whisk together the molasses and melted butter and beat into the egg-sugar mixture.
4. In a small bowl, stir together the flour, baking soda, ginger, cinnamon, cardamom, cloves, nutmeg and pepper. Add to the liquid mixture and combine on low speed, then increase speed and beat on high until well incorporated and a little lighter in color.
5. Pour into the prepared pan. Bake until the cake springs back when very lightly touched and is just beginning to pull from the sides of the pan, about 25 minutes. Cool on a rack until the cake is cool enough to handle, then cut into 2-inch squares.

For the Bread Pudding Soak:
1. Meanwhile, in a saucepan over medium heat, combine the heavy cream, half and half and sugar. Split open the vanilla bean lengthwise and scrape the seeds into the pot. Add the bean. Heat, stirring occasionally, until steaming. Do not boil. When the cream is hot, remove the pot from the heat.
2. Meanwhile, whisk the yolks together in a small bowl. Whisk a little of the hot cream mixture into the yolks until warmed, and then whisk the yolk mixture back into the cream.
3. Pour through a strainer into a large glass measuring cup or a mixing bowl.
4. Preheat oven to 300°F. Bring a kettle of water to boil. Spray a 9-inch baking pan with cooking spray or line with parchment paper. Stack the gingerbread squares in a double layer, cutting pieces as necessary to fit them all in the pan. Pour the warm bread pudding soak over the gingerbread, allowing it to seep into the edges and cracks.
5. Place the pan inside a larger pan, and pour hot water into the larger pan until it comes about three-fourths up the side of the bread pudding pan. Bake the pudding in the water bath until firmly set, abut 3½ hours. Serve with Meyer Lemon Curd.

For the Lemon Curd:
1. In the top of a double boiler over 1-inch of water, whisk together the sugar, zest, lemon juice, egg and yolk. Cook, stirring regularly, until thickened.
2. Remove from heat and strain into a medium bowl. Slowly whisk in the butter, a few tbsp. at a time, until well incorporated.

JCT. KITCHEN
1198 HOWELL MILL ROAD N.W.

"Gingers are chewing gum for the eyes."
Frank Lloyd Wright

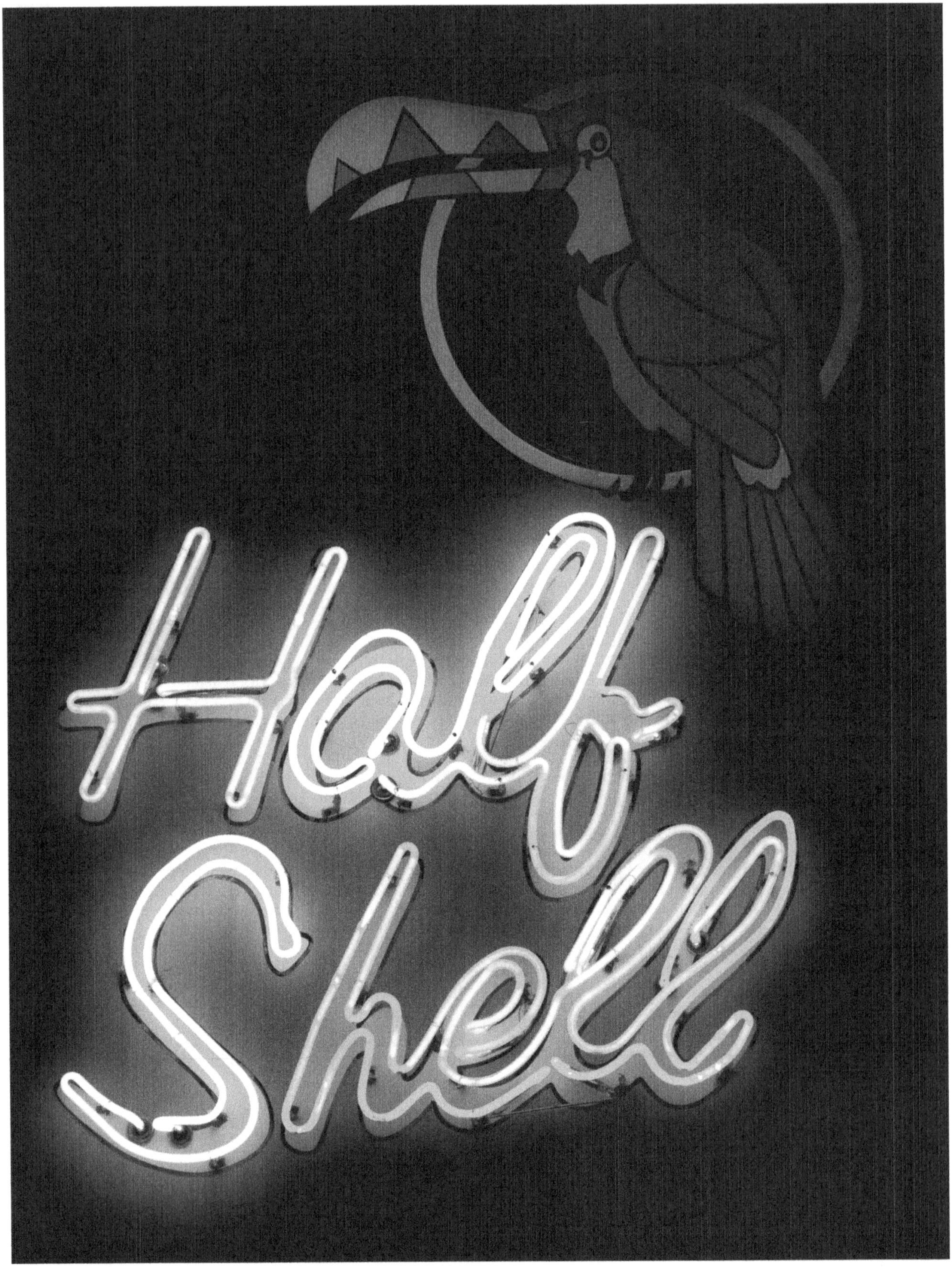
Half
Shell

WATERCRESS-RANCH SALAD DRESSING

Ms. Strickland writes: "After dining at Jim White's Half Shell for at least 20 years, I was finally able to persuade our regular server to get the salad dressing recipe for me. She went to the kitchen and came back a few minutes later, relating how the dressing was made. This is what I was told: She watched the cook pour the contents of a large Hidden Valley Ranch Salad Dressing Mix packet into the blender, following the instructions on the package, and threw in a handful of fresh watercress. I was shocked that it could be so easy, but when I tried it at home, it was, in fact, the same dressing. I've been making it for years."

1 (.4-oz.) packet Hidden Valley Ranch buttermilk salad dressing mix
1 C. buttermilk
1 C. mayonnaise
1 C. watercress leaves

1. In a blender, combine salad dressing mix, buttermilk, mayonnaise and watercress and pulse to combine. Refrigerate dresing until ready to use.

JIM WHITE'S HALF SHELL
2349 PEACHTREE RD.

"It takes four men to dress a salad: a wise man for the salt, a madman for the pepper, a miser for the vinegar, and a spendthrift for the oil."
Anonymous

JOLI-KOBE
Bakery & Café

OPEN

GINGER DRESSING

Signature Tastes of ATLANTA

Joli Kobe Bakery: "Joli," as in the French for "pretty," and "Kobe" for the Japanese city from which the store's owner hails. The bakery started turning out croissants to chocolate eclairs in 1985 before closing in 2001 for renovation and expansion. Now at twice the size of the original bakery and with a large-scale pastry-baking kitchen downstairs, Joli Kobe, run by chef François Collet, is filled with traditional French pastries and desserts from mousses to madeleines.

2 tsp. chopped fresh ginger
1½ tsp. finely chopped yellow onion
1 small clove garlic
¾ tsp. yellow mustard
¼ C. aji-mirin or mirin (sweetened rice wine)
2 tbsp. soy sauce plus more for seasoning
2 tbsp. water
1 C. vegetable oil
salt and pepper, to taste

1. Place the ginger, onion, garlic, yellow mustard, aji-mirin and soy sauce in the blender and blend until smooth.

2. Add the water and, with the motor running, gradually add the vegetable oil in a thin stream.

3. Season to taste with salt, pepper and soy sauce.

5600 ROSWELL ROAD N.E.

JOLI KOBE

"Be a ginger of quality. Some people aren't used to an environment where excellence is expected."
Steve Jobs

129

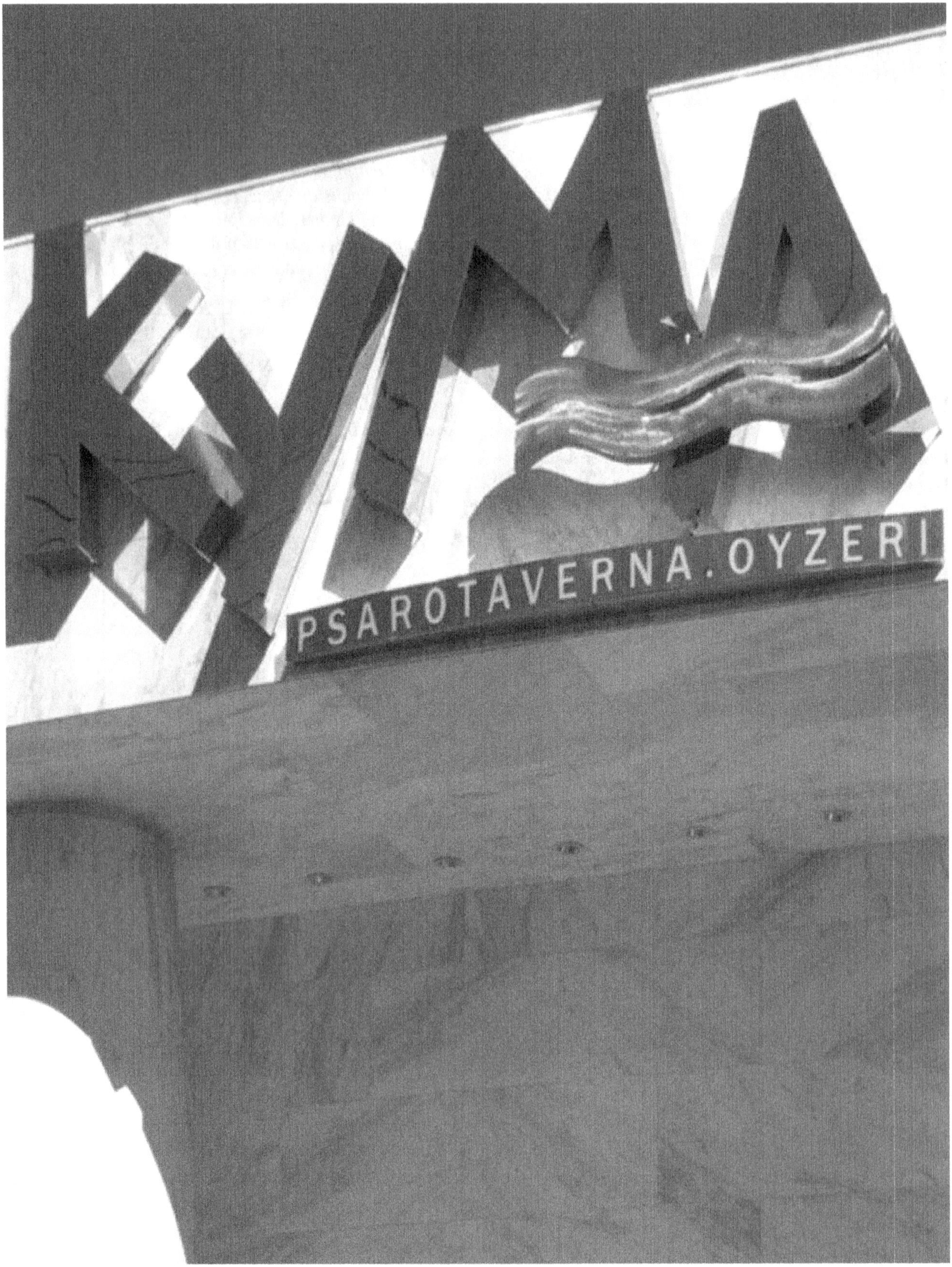
PSAROTAVERNA.OYZERI

MELITZANOSALATA

Kyma is a contemporary seafood tavern with an inventive yet approachable menu that stays true to its Mediterranean origins. Kyma's dazzling constellation display on the deep blue ceiling, white marble columns and bold fresh fish display are dramatic while the inviting patio offers an ideal setting for savoring a glass of Greek wine. Fresh, healthy food, attentive Mediterranean hospitality and festive atmosphere await at Kyma.

4 lb. of eggplant
½ C. extra virgin olive oil, plus extra for rubbing
salt
2 tsp. thick yogurt
⅓ C. good-quality red wine vinegar
1 garlic clove, minced
4 fresh mint leaves, thinly sliced
⅓ C. chopped fresh parsley
2½ C. finely chopped walnuts
¼ red onion, finely diced
freshly ground black pepper

1. Preheat a grill to medium-high.

2. Pierce eggplants with a fork, rub with olive oil and sprinkle with salt. Place on hot grill.

3. Grill eggplants, turning every 5-10 minutes, until the inner flesh has totally collapsed, about 30 minutes, depending on the size of the eggplants. Remove from grill and cool for 1-1 ½ hours.

4. When cool, cut each eggplant in half and carefully scoop out all flesh with a spoon. Discard skin and large clusters of seeds. Pass the eggplant flesh through a food mill or puree in a food processor. Transfer eggplant to cheesecloth and hang in cheesecloth overnight.

5. In a large bowl, place drained eggplant puree. Fold in olive oil, yogurt, red wine vinegar, garlic, mint, parsley, walnuts and onion. Season with salt and pepper.

3085 PIEDMONT ROAD

KYMA

"I'm nuts and I know it. But so long as I make 'em laugh, they ain't going to lock me up."
Red Skelton

Fettuccine con Pollo alla Padella

La Grotta, in Atlanta for over thirty years, has earned a reputation for elegant dining and gracious, hospitable service. We are pleased that our location at the Ravinia complex in Dunwoody also enjoys the accolades of our tradition. Both restaurants have been singled out and honored with the prestigious AAA Four Diamond Award and the DiRONA Award every year since 1993.

1 lb. fettuccine
2 tbsp. butter
3 boneless, skinless chicken breasts
½ C. bleached all-purpose flour
3 tbsp. extra virgin olive oil
3 cloves garlic, sliced lengthwise
4 Roma tomatoes, peeled, seeded and chopped
1 C. low-sodium chicken stock
1 C. (2 sticks) unsalted butter
½ C. fresh parmesan cheese
¼ lb. spinach
salt and pepper, to taste

1. Prepare pasta according to package directions and set aside.

2. Meanwhile, in a medium sauté pan over medium heat, melt 2 tbsp. butter. Lightly "dust" chicken breasts in flour and cook for 5-10 minutes, turning regularly.

3. Remove chicken from the pan and set aside to cool. When cool enough to handle, slice into strips and re-serve.

4. In a large sauté pan, heat oil.

5. Add garlic and sauté until softened.

6. Add tomatoes and chicken stock. Bring to a boil and cook for 4-5 minutes, until partially reduced. Reduce the heat to low and add the butter, stir until melted.

7. Add the reserved chicken and fettuccine, parmesan and spinach and toss gently to combine. When spinach has wilted, add salt and pepper to taste and serve immediately.

CROWNE PLAZA RAVINIA, 4355 ASHFORD DUNWOODY ROAD

LA GROTTA

"Cook ingredients that you are used to cooking by other techniques, such as fish, chicken, or hamburgers. In other words be comfortable with the ingredients you are using."
Bobby Flay

TRATTORÌA

la Tavola

VEAL AND SPINACH MANICOTTI

Signature Tastes of ATLANTA

This rendition of the Italian favorite comes from Joey Masi's mother, Francesca. Masi is the consulting chef who developed the menu at La Tavola, which is becoming the local trattoria in the Virginia-Highland neighborhood. Typically, manicotti is is filled with meat or cheese. Buon appetito from La Tavola!

1 tbsp. vegetable oil
1 medium yellow onion, diced
1 tbsp. chopped garlic, about 5 to 6 cloves
1 lb. ground veal
1 lb. frozen chopped spinach, thawed and drained
1¼ C. shredded mozzarella cheese, divided
salt and pepper, to taste
½ lb. fresh pasta sheets or prepared manicotti shells (about 12 shells)
2 C. tomato sauce, divided
3 tbsp. grated parmesan cheese
3 tbsp. chopped parsley

1. Preheat oven to 375°F and lightly grease a 9x13-inch baking pan.

2. Heat oil in a large skillet over medium-high heat. Sauté onion and garlic until translucent, about 5 minutes.

3. Add ground veal and sauté until veal has browned.

4. Add chopped spinach and cook for 10 minutes. Remove from heat and let cool slightly.

5. Add 1 cup mozzarella and mix thoroughly. Add salt and pepper to taste.

6. Put a 4x3-inch pasta sheet on cutting board. Place 2 to 3 tbsp. of veal filling on pasta and roll into a tube. Repeat process with remaining sheets and filling.

7. Place ¾ cup tomato sauce in the bottom of the dish. Arrange the manicotti in the dish on top of sauce. Place remaining tomato sauce on manicotti and sprinkle with remaining mozzarella, grated parmesan and chopped parsley.

8. Cover loosely with aluminum foil and bake for 15 to 20 minutes or until cheese has melted.

LA TAVOLA
992 VIRGINIA AVE.

"It's like eating your spinach or going to the gym. At first it hurts, but over the long term, investors are getting better information and companies are guarding themselves against a disaster. That's good for everyone."
Matt Kelly

LEBANESE RICE PUDDING

Visit Lawrence's Cafe and experience an evening of wonderful food, fine wine, and delicious pastries. Lawrence's Cafe specializes in Lebanese cuisine. Everything on the menu is prepared from scratch with the finest ingredients by Chef Tony. Lawrence's Cafe is available for private parties on Sundays and offers take out and catering services.

Signature Tastes of ATLANTA

¼ C. white rice
3 C. 2% milk
¾ C. rice flour
1½ C. granulated sugar
1 scant tsp. rose water
½ tbsp. ground pistachios

1. Bring ½ cup water to a boil in a medium saucepan.

2. Add the white rice and boil until tender, about 20 minutes.

3. Add the milk and return to a boil, then stir in rice flour to thicken.

4. Remove from heat. Add sugar and whisk well.

5. Refrigerate until ready to serve. Pudding will thicken as it chills.

6. When ready to serve, add the rose water and mix well. Pour into individual cups. Top each serving with ground pistachios.

LAWRENCE'S CAFE AND RESTAURANT

2888 BUFORD HIGHWAY NORTHEAST

"The proof is in the pudding when they come home. Will we have the data about their health, will we know where they were stationed, what their unit deployments were? I will need that information."
Anthony Principi

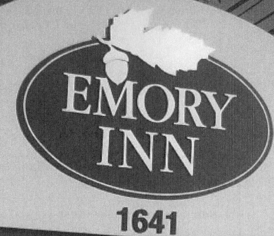

EMORY
INN

1641

le giverny

Sweet Potato Bisque

Signature Taste of ATLANTA

2 tbsp. olive oil
1 onion, diced
1 large carrot, peeled and diced
4 celery ribs, finely chopped
6 whole garlic cloves, chopped
1 tsp. salt
1 tsp. ground black pepper
½ tsp. dry oregano
½ tsp. curry powder
½ tsp. ground cumin
½ tsp. ground coriander
¼ tsp. ground cinnamon
½ C. white wine
5 large sweet potatoes, peeled and diced into 1-inch cubes
6-8 C. chicken stock
1 bouquet garni (1 or 2 bay leaves, 2 cloves, 10 branches of fresh thyme, 10 parsley stalks, wrapped in cheesecloth tied with kitchen twine)
½ C. heavy cream
¼ C. (½ stick) butter
½ tsp. vanilla extract
2-3 tbsp. honey, or to taste

1. In a large stockpot, heat the oil over medium heat. Add the onion, carrot, celery, garlic, salt and pepper. Cook 3 minutes to sweat the vegetables. Add the oregano, curry powder, cumin, coriander and cinnamon. Cook another 3 minutes or until fragrant, stirring often to make sure the vegetables do not stick to the bottom of the pan.

2. Add the white wine and cook 1 minute. Add the sweet potatoes and enough chicken stock to cover all the vegetables. Add the bouquet garni. Cover the pot and simmer until the sweet potatoes are very tender, about 20 to 30 minutes. Remove the bouquet garni.

3. Carefully puree the soup in batches in a blender until very smooth (use caution when blending hot liquids; do not fill the blender more than halfway).

4. Strain through a fine strainer and return the soup to the pot over medium-low heat. Add the heavy cream. If the soup is too thick, add additional hot stock or water. Add the butter, stirring constantly until fully incorporated. Add more salt and pepper to taste. Add the vanilla extract. Stir in honey to taste.

Le Giverny Bistro
1641 Clifton Road N.E.

"My idea of heaven is a great big baked potato and someone to share it with."
Oprah Winfrey

SPAGHETTINI FRA DIAVOLO CON SCAMPI

Marcella Hazan, the renowned cookbook author and grande dame of Italian cooking, is the creator of this version of the spicy Italian standard. Salvatore Medina, who trained under Hazan, added it to the menu at Lombardi's when he became the chef.

*salt, to taste
6 oz. dried spaghettini, about 3 C. cooked
½ C. extra virgin olive oil
3 cloves garlic
1 lb. fresh ripe plum tomatoes, peeled, seeded and diced
½ tsp. dried basil
½ tsp. dried oregano
½ lb. large shrimp, peeled and deveined
freshly ground black pepper, to taste
pinch or more dried red pepper flakes*

1. Bring 2 quarts of salted water to a boil in a large pot.

2. When water is boiling, add pasta and stir until strands are completely submerged. Cook 6-8 minutes until al dente. Drain and keep warm until sauce is ready.

3. Heat olive oil in a large skillet over medium heat. Add garlic and stir for 2 minutes, until it just begins to turn golden brown.

4. Increase heat to medium-high and add the tomatoes. Cook until most of the liquid has evaporated, about 6 minutes.

5. Add basil, oregano and shrimp to skillet. Season with salt and pepper to taste and cook just until shrimp turn pink, 5-6 minutes.

6. Add the sauce to the warm pasta and toss well. Sprinkle with dried red pepper flakes and serve.

LOMBARDI'S
94 UPPER PRYOR ST. S.W.

"I think my character's getting to the point where he can't even eat spaghetti with red sauce anymore, where he has horrible nightmares, he can't sleep anymore.
George Eads

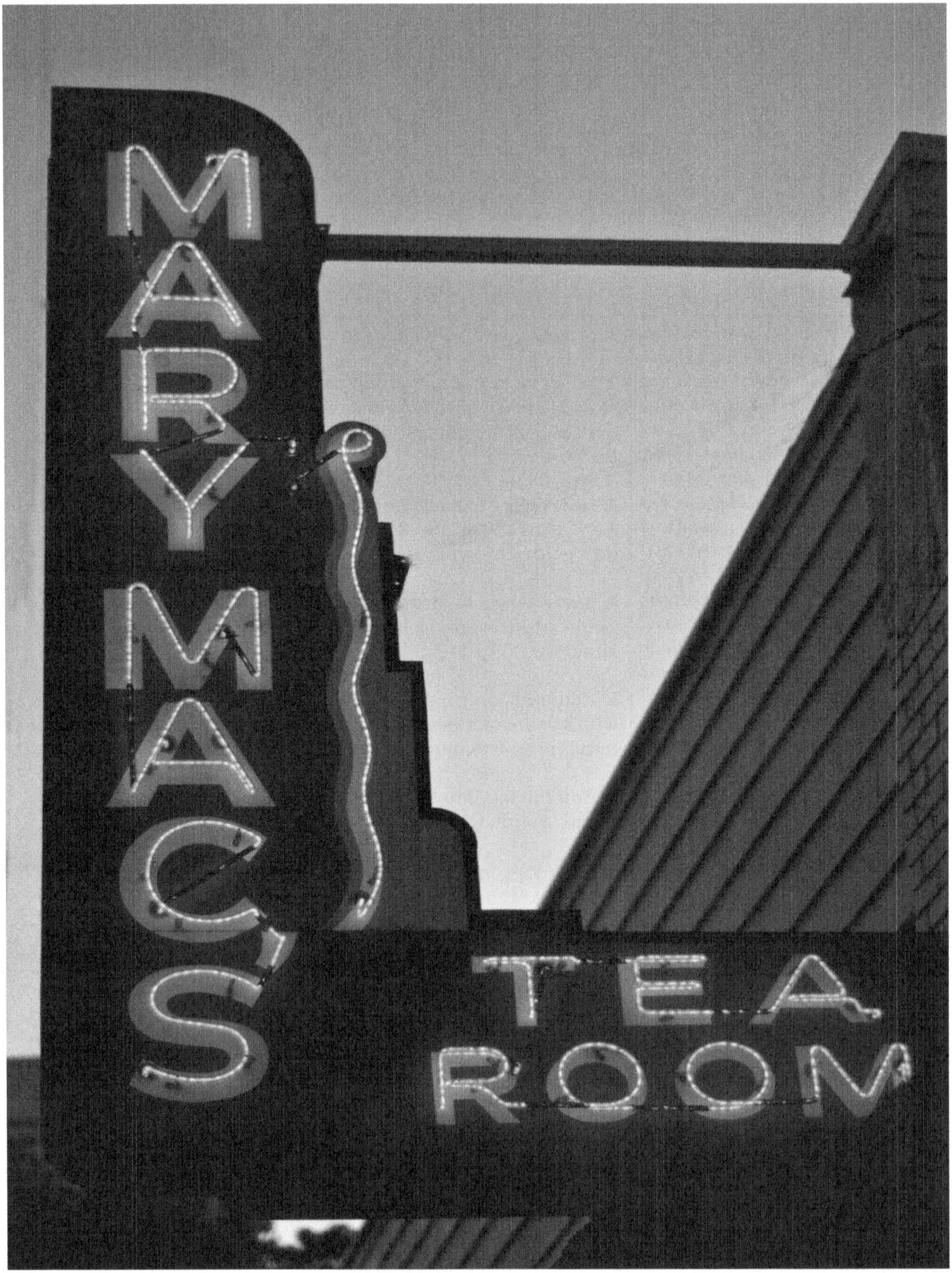
MARY MAC'S
TEA
ROOM

TEA ROOM FRIED CHICKEN

Mary Mac's Tea Room opened in 1945, today it is the last of sixteen tea rooms that once dotted intown Atlanta in the 1940s. We believe we are still here 65 years later because we focus on serving made-from-scratch true Southern fare served with genuine Southern hospitality. From the time you come in the door you're welcomed with open arms and a big smile.

Signature Tastes of ATLANTA

1 (3-3½ lb.) chicken, cut into 8 pcs.
4 tsp. salt, divided
2 tsp. white pepper, divided
peanut oil
1 C. water
3 C. all-purpose flour, divided

1. Sprinkle chicken with 1 tsp. salt and ½ teaspoon white pepper. Refrigerate for 1 hour.

2. In a deep fryer or large stockpot, pour enough peanut oil to come halfway up the sides. Heat oil to 325°F over medium-high heat.

3. In a medium mixing bowl, combine water, 1 cup flour, 1 teaspoon salt and ½ teaspoon white pepper.

4. In a separate bowl, combine 2 cups all-purpose flour, 2 teaspoons salt and 1 teaspoon white pepper.

5. Dip chicken pieces into wet batter first then coat with flour mixture.

6. Carefully add chicken to hot oil. Chicken should be fully submerged in oil. Fry chicken for about 18 to 20 minutes.

7. Drain chicken on a wire cooling rack set over a rimmed baking sheet.

MARY MAC'S TEA ROOM
224 PONCE DE LEON AVE

"Cutting up fowl to predict the future is, if done honestly and with as little interpretation as possible, a kind of randomization. But chicken guts are hard to read and invite flights of fancy or corruption."
Ian Hacking

Mirage Salad

Located in the heart of Sandy Springs since 1997, Mirage is the oldest Persian restaurant in the Atlanta area. The healthy delicious style of Persian cooking awaits you at Mirage where we celebrate good food and authentic Persian cuisine with pride every day. From our succulent and mouth watering variety of beef, lamb, chicken, and seafood kebabs to our glorious and tasty mixed rice dishes, you are sure to find something on our menu to meet your high culinary expectations.

½ C. slivered dried orange peel, or the zest of 3 oranges
½ C. granulated sugar
⅛ tsp. ground saffron
2 tbsp. extra virgin olive oil
½ C. slivered almonds
½ C. halved raw pistachios
1 C. julienne carrots, cut ⅛-inch thick
8 C. torn romaine lettuce
½ C. shredded red cabbage
1 C. cherry tomatoes
½ C. dried currants or small raisins
½ C. dried barberries
¼ C. red wine vinaigrette
salt and pepper

1. Soak the orange peel in cold water for 2 hours; drain. Boil orange peels in fresh water for 5 minutes; drain and repeat. Bring 1 C. water to boil, add the sugar and stir until it dissolves, then add the blanched orange peels and boil until the water has completely evaporated. Set candied orange peels aside.

2. Stir saffron into 2 tbsp. of boiling water; set aside.

3. In a small skillet, heat the olive oil over medium heat. Add the almonds and pistachios and sauté for 2 minutes.

4. Add the carrots and candied orange peel and sauté until nuts are lightly brown, about 2 minutes.

5. Stir in the saffron water and remove the pan from the heat. Cool the mixture to room temperature.

6. Arrange the lettuce and red cabbage in a serving bowl. Top with tomatoes, currants, barberries and the cooled nut mixture. Toss with the red wine vinaigrette. Season to taste with salt and pepper.

"My salad days—When I was green in judgment"
William Shakespeare

KOBE BEEF SLIDERS

Mosaic is a neighborhood bistro that showcases modern American cuisine in a cozy setting, worth returning to again and again. Located on a quaint, tucked-away side street in Buckhead, Mosaic exudes charm at first glance. Mosaic promises to provide fantastic casual American food, personalized service and an engaging atmosphere.

Soy Ginger Glaze:
1 C. soy sauce
2 tbsp. granulated sugar
juice of ½ lemon
juice of ½ lime
juice of ½ orange
3 oz. (¼ C. plus 2 tbsp.) pineapple juice
1 oz. fresh peeled ginger, chopped
3 green onions, white part only, chopped

Soy Ginger Mayo:
½ C. mayonnaise
1 tbsp. Soy Ginger Glaze

Sliders:
1 lb. high-quality ground beef, such as Kobe
1 tbsp. Soy Ginger Glaze
1½ tsp. onion powder
1½ tsp. garlic powder
1 tsp. curry powder
½ tsp. ground cumin
3 green onions, green part only, chopped
12 small rolls, such as Hawaiian sweet rolls, sliced in half
12 thin, 1-inch slices chilled triple-cream brie cheese

For the Soy Ginger Glaze:

1. In a saucepan over medium-high heat, combine soy sauce, sugar, lemon, lime, orange and pineapple juices, ginger and green onions.

2. Cook until mixture is reduced by half. When a spoon is dipped into the mixture, it should coat the spoon. Strain the liquid and discard the solids. Set aside. Makes about ½ cup.

For the Soy Ginger Mayo:

1. In a bowl, combine the mayonnaise and glaze. Chill until ready to use.

For the Sliders:

1. Preheat oven to 300°F. Preheat the grill or a griddle.

2. In a mixing bowl, combine the beef, Soy Ginger Glaze, onion powder, garlic powder, curry powder, cumin and green onions. Form the beef into 12 patties. Set aside.

3. Place the bottom half of the rolls, cut side up, on a serving platter and dress with 1 tsp. of Soy Ginger Mayo. Place the top half of the rolls, cut side up, on a baking sheet and top with the cheese slices. Heat the rolls and cheese in the oven until the cheese is softened, about 5 minutes.

4. Meanwhile, grill or sear the patties until desired doneness. Place the patties on the bottom half of the buns, brush with Soy Ginger Glaze and top with other half of the bun.

MOSAIC RESTAURANT
3097 MAPLE DRIVE

"A hamburger by any other name costs twice as much."
Evan Esar

SWEET AND SOUR MANGO CHICKEN

MuLan offers creative dinner entrees that you won't find at most Chinese restaurants. Were located in the trendy area of Midtown in a beautifully renovated Victorian house. MuLan offers both downstairs and private upstairs dining area as well as an outdoor patio. MuLan specializes in preparing gourmet, authentic Chinese dishes with an emphasis on seafood.

Signature Tastes of ATLANTA

¾ C. mango juice
¾ C. pineapple juice
¼ C. apple cider vinegar
1 C. granulated sugar
4 tsp. cornstarch
¾ C. cold water
vegetable oil for frying
1 C. rice flour
1 tsp. salt
2 lb. skinless, boneless chicken breasts, cut into bite-size pieces
1½ C. fresh or frozen mixed fruit, such as mango slices, peach slices, pineapple chunks and strawberries

1. In a medium saucepan over medium-high heat, combine the mango juice, pineapple juice, vinegar and sugar. Bring to a simmer.

2. Stir the cornstarch into the cold water until the cornstarch dissolves, then slowly pour it into the juice mixture, stirring constantly. Bring the liquid back to a simmer. Stir until the mixture thickens and clarifies, about 2 minutes. Set aside.

3. In a fryer or heavy saucepan, heat at least 1-inch of vegetable oil to 350°F.

4. In a plastic bag, combine the rice flour and salt. Drop the chicken pieces into the flour, close the bag and shake until the chicken pieces are thoroughly coated.

5. Working in batches, place the dredged chicken pieces in the hot oil and cook until golden, 2-3 minutes. Drain the chicken pieces on paper towel.

6. Return the mango sauce to a simmer. Add the cooked chicken pieces and fruit and stir to combine. Serve over rice.

824 JUNIPER ST. N.E.

MU LAN

"The fact that it's such an aggressive beetle toward mango crops, and South Florida is the No. 1 mango growing area in the United States, we were very lucky to catch this."
Jennifer Connors

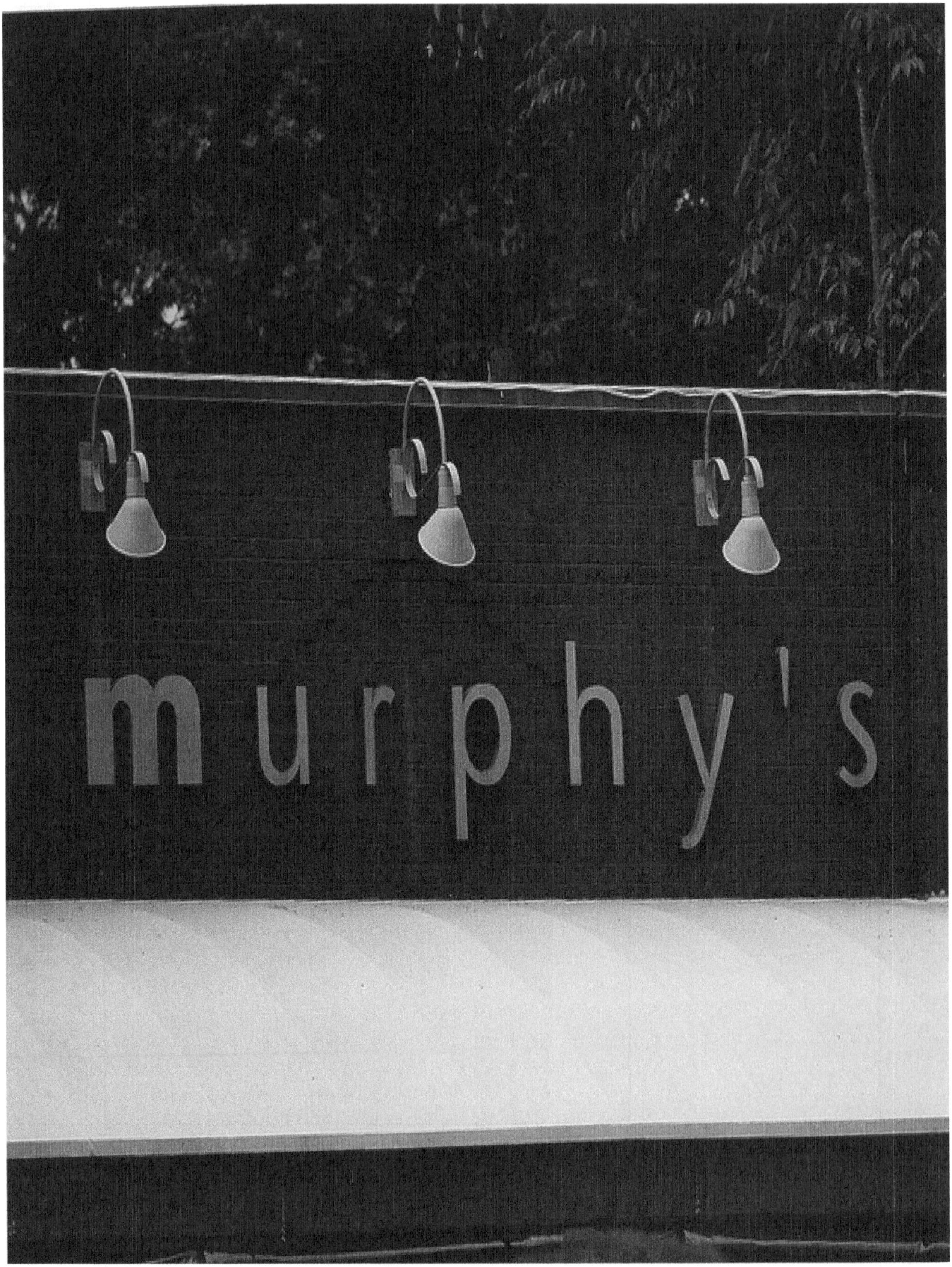
murphy's

Murphy's is one of Atlanta's best-loved restaurants and has been for the past 30 years. Located in the heart of stylish Virginia Highland, Murphy's is the long-standing hub of neighborhood camaraderie and the choice destination for visitors seeking the best of the district's dining and nightlife. Tom Murphy's acclaimed restaurant brings in the crowds with the perfect combination of upscale comfort food, gracious service, a cozy setting, and excellent value.

Brownie:
shortening for the pan
1 C. (2 sticks) margarine
½ C. semisweet chocolate morsels
1⅓ C. cake flour
⅓ C. cocoa
2 C. granulated sugar
3 eggs
1 tsp. vanilla extract

Cheesecake:
3 (8-oz.) packages plus 2 tbsp. cream cheese
1⅓ C. granulated sugar
5 eggs
1 tsp. vanilla extract

Chocolate Mousse:
14 oz. semisweet chocolate
1½ C. whipped cream
9 egg yolks (from pasteurized eggs)
½ C. granulated sugar

For the Brownie:
1. Grease a 10-inch springform pan. Preheat oven to 300°F.
2. In a small saucepan over medium-low heat, melt margarine. Add chocolate morsels, stirring often.
3. In a large mixing bowl, combine flour, cocoa, sugar, eggs and vanilla; mix well.
4. Pour chocolate mixture into flour mixture. Scrape down sides and bottom of the bowl and mix well.
5. Pour batter into prepared pan. Bake 1 hour. Remove from oven and let cool to room temperature.

For the Cheesecake:
1. Bring cream cheese to room temperature. Preheat oven to 300°F.
2. In a mixing bowl, combine the cream cheese and sugar. Add eggs and vanilla.
3. Pour mixture over cooled brownie layer and bake, checking after 45 minutes. If it is not set, continue baking up to 15 minutes until set. Remove and set aside to cool.

For the Chocolate Mousse:
1. Melt chocolate in a double boiler and keep warm.
2. Whip cream and set aside.
3. Beat egg yolks until they are doubled in volume. Add sugar and hot melted chocolate at medium speed. Immediately fold in whipped cream.
4. Spread chocolate mousse over cooled cheesecake.
5. Chill at least 2 hours before serving.

"A page of my journal is like a cake of portable soup. A little may be diffused into a considerable portion."
James Boswell

Nam's Shaken Beef

Chris and Alex Kinjo, along with their mother, are proud to present Taste of Nam at their MF Buckhead restaurant. The family is bringing back the exotic ingredients and spices of their popular former Midtown restaurant, Nam, often recognized and awarded as the best Vietnamese cuisine in Atlanta. The exclusive Taste of Nam dining experience is now offered twice per month at a premier Buckhead location; the world class Terminus office towers, at the corner of Piedmont and Peachtree Rd.

1 tsp. soy sauce
1 tsp. oyster sauce
1 tsp. fresh garlic, minced
½ tsp. ground black pepper
½ tsp. granulated sugar
1 lb. filet mignon, cut into 1-inch cubes
2 tsp. vegetable oil

1. In a large bowl, combine soy sauce, oyster sauce, garlic, black pepper and sugar. Add filet mignon and toss to coat. Marinate for 10 minutes.

2. In a large skillet over high heat, add oil.

3. When skillet is very hot, add beef and marinade and sauté or shake for 1-2 minutes, turning the meat to quickly cook the outside but barely cook the inside.

931 Monroe Drive

NAM

"If I could only have one type of food with me, I would bring soy sauce. The reason being that if I have soy sauce, I can flavor a lot of things. "
Martin Yan

PECAN PIE MUFFINS

Nancy Goodrich, aka Nancy G, admits she has a muffin fan base. "We started serving muffins for brunch, and they were so popular that we started serving them every day at lunch," she said. The pecan flavor does taste like a cross between a muffin and pie – sweet, but crumbly-tender. Stored in an air-tight container, they keep well for a few days, too.

**1 C. firmly packed light brown sugar
1 C. chopped pecans
½ C. all-purpose flour
½ tsp. baking powder
¼ tsp. salt
½ C. butter, melted
2 large eggs, lightly beaten
1 tsp. vanilla extract**

1. Preheat oven to 425°F. Lightly grease (or coat with nonstick cooking spray) 3 miniature muffin pans.

2. In a large bowl, combine the brown sugar, pecans, flour, baking powder and salt. Make a well in the center of the mixture.

3. In a small bowl, mix together the butter, eggs and vanilla.

4. Pour the wet ingredients into the dry ingredients and stir just until combined. Spoon the batter evenly into the miniature muffin pans, filling each compartment ¾ full. (Fill any empty compartments halfway with water to prevent damage to the pan.) Bake for 8-10 minutes, until lightly browned. Makes about 30 muffins.

NANCY G'S CAFE
4920 ROSWELL RD # 55

"Pie is a symbol of something bigger than Mom and her way with desserts."
Pasquale Le Draqulec

PERFECT MARGARITA

Located in the heart of Buckhead, Nava offers a Southwestern experience with flavorful cuisine, bold design and striking architecture. Nava's innovative and flavorful menu has intense Latin influences. Enjoy one of our signature margaritas in the inviting bar, or relax on our award-winning garden-side patio. Friendly and attentive service makes your experience unforgettably fun at Nava.

¼ C. granulated sugar
2 tbsp. water
½ C. fresh lemon juice
½ C. fresh lime juice
½ C. plus 2 tbsp. Sauza Anejo Conmemorativo tequila
¼ C. Cointreau
course salt

1. To make a simple syrup, stir sugar and water together in a saucepan and heat until sugar is dissolved and liquid is clear. Set aside to cool.

2. Pour the tequila and Cointreau into a pitcher, then stir in the simple syrup.

3. Add lemon and lime juices and stir.

4. Pour over ice into salted margarita glasses. (To salt glasses, rub rims with a lemon or lime wedge, then dip into salt.)

3060 PEACHTREE ROAD

NAVA

"I want to make lemonade out of the lemons that were dealt to me."
Baron Hill

SHEPHERD'S PIE

The New American Shakespeare Tavern is unlike other theaters. It is a place out of time; a place of live music, hand-crafted period costumes, outrageous sword fights with the entire experience centered on the passion and poetry of the spoken word. With an authentic British Pub Menu and a broad selection of Irish ales and premium brews, the Shakespeare Tavern is a place to eat, drink, and nourish the soul.

Signature Tastes of ATLANTA

For the Filling:
1 tbsp., plus 2 tsp. vegetable oil, divided
2 C. diced onions
2 large carrots, peeled, cut in half lengthwise and then into 1-inch chunks
½ bunch fresh celery, chopped
2 cloves garlic, minced
2¼ lb. beef chuck roast, trimmed and cut into 1-inch chunks
salt and pepper
⅔ C. white wine, divided
1 C. low-sodium chicken broth, divided
2 tbsp. Worcestershire sauce
1½ tsp. fresh thyme, minced, divided
2 tbsp. fresh rosemary, minced, divided
¼ C. cornstarch

For the Topping:
2½ lb. russet potatoes, unpeeled and scrubbed
¼ C. (½ stick) butter
6 cloves garlic, minced
salt and pepper

1. Preheat oven to 350°F.
2. In an ovenproof Dutch oven, heat 1 tablespoon oil over medium heat. Add the onion, carrots, celery and garlic and cook until the vegetables begin to soften.
3. Meanwhile, heat a 12-inch skillet over high heat. Add 1 teaspoon vegetable oil and swirl to cover the pan. Sprinkle the beef with salt and pepper. When the oil is shimmering but not smoking, add half the beef and brown on all sides, then add the beef to the Dutch oven with the vegetables.
4. Pour ⅓ cup of the white wine into the skillet and cook over high heat until reduced by half, scraping up any browned bits. Pour the reduction into the Dutch oven.
5. Repeat the browning process with remaining oil and beef, and repeat the wine reduction, adding both to the Dutch oven.
6. Pour ¾ cup of the chicken broth and the Worcestershire sauce into the Dutch oven, and add half the minced thyme and rosemary, reserving the remaining chicken broth and herbs.
7. Stir the beef mixture well and bring to a simmer on top of the stove. Cover, place in oven for 1½ hours.
8. While the beef is cooking, start the potatoes. Boil the whole potatoes in plenty of water until they are easily pierced with a fork, about 45 minutes.
9. Pour off the water and let the potatoes sit, off heat, until they are cool enough to handle. Press the potatoes through a potato ricer, or peel and mash them by hand. Set aside
10. Melt the butter in a small saucepan. Add the minced garlic and cook for 30 seconds, then remove from heat.
11. Pour the melted garlic butter into the potatoes, season with salt and pepper to taste, and beat the potatoes with a whisk until they are light and fluffy. Cover and keep warm.
12. After 1½ hours, check the beef for tenderness—it should be just about falling apart.
13. Stir the cornstarch into the reserved (cold) chicken broth, and stir the mixture into the hot beef. Stir in the remaining rosemary and thyme, and continue stirring until the mixture has thickened.
14. Pour the beef mixture into a 9x13-inch baking dish. Spread the mashed potatoes over the top, return to the oven and bake for 30 minutes until hot and bubbly.

NEW AMERICAN SHAKESPEARE TAVERN
499 PEACHTREE STREET NORTHEAST

"Pie is the food of the heroic. No pie eating nation can ever be vanquished."
NY Times

Almond Macaroons

Since 1976, Nikolai's Roof, located on the 30th floor of the Hilton Atlanta, has impressed patrons and restaurant critics with its masterfully prepared French and Russian dishes by Chef Olivier de Brusschere, panoramic views of the Atlanta skyline, enchanting ambiance and impeccable dining staff. Nikolai's Roof has been the recipient of the highly coveted AAA Four Diamond award for over 20 consecutive years and is the longest standing restaurant in Atlanta to do so.

8 oz. almond paste
⅓ C. granulated sugar
1½ C. confectioners' sugar
¼ C. all-purpose flour
2 egg whites

1. Preheat oven to 350°F. Line baking sheets with parchment paper.

2. In a mixer fitted with a paddle attachment, mix almond paste, both sugars, flour and egg whites until well-blended and smooth.

3. Pipe 1-inch rounds onto a paper-lined pan using a plain piping tip fitted in a pastry bag.

4. With damp fingertips, press down any peaks. Bake until lightly golden, about 10-12 minutes. Allow to cool on pans before removing from paper.

Signature Tastes of ATLANTA

NIKOLAI'S ROOF
255 COURTLAND ST.

"A wise woman puts a grain of sugar into everything she says to a man, and takes a grain of salt with everything he says to her."
Helen Rowland

Orecchiette con Granchio

Signature Tastes of ATLANTA

Nino's, opened in 1968, has been owned and operated by Antonio Noviello since 1982. Originally from the Amalfi Coast of southern Italy, Antonio worked in Monte Carlo, then Bermuda where he met his wife Helen, an Atlanta resident. After moving to Atlanta in 1981, Antonio's life-long dream of owning his own restaurant became a reality when he purchased Nino's.

1 lb. orecchiette pasta
1 tsp. butter
1 rib celery, diced small
2 carrots, diced
1 tsp. green peppercorns
½ C. brandy
½ lb. lump crab meat
3 C. heavy whipping cream

1. Bring a large pot of salted water to boil. Cook pasta al dente and drain.

2. While pasta cooks, heat butter in a large saucepan over medium-high heat. Sauté the celery and carrots until hot, 1-2 minutes.

3. Add the green peppercorns, brandy, crab meat and cream. Bring mixture to a light boil. Remove from heat and toss with the pasta.

1931 Cheshire Bridge Road N.E.

Nino's

"Give us this day our daily taste. Restore to us soups that spoons will not sink in and sauces which are never the same twice. Raise up among us stews with more gravy than we have bread to blot it with Give us pasta with a hundred fillings."
Robert Farrar Capon

Noche, located at the corner of Virginia and North Highland, is the perfect place to meet your friends and enjoy some famous margaritas and Spanish influence tapas. The high energy bar is a huge crowd pleaser. Locals love to pack themselves into this hot spot nightly! Noche has been voted best margaritas by Jezebel magazine. Noche is open nightly for dinner and Saturday and Sunday for lunch.

3 C. low-sodium chicken stock
2 C. half and half
2 C. heavy cream
1 C. grits
½ C. masa harina
3 ears yellow corn, grilled or roasted and cut off the cob
salt and pepper

1. In a large pot, bring the chicken broth, half and half and heavy cream to boil.

2. Reduce the heat and slowly stir in the grits and masa. Continue stirring, pressing out any lumps, until thickened, about 20 minutes.

3. Add corn and stir to combine. Season with salt and pepper to taste.

1000 VIRGINIA AVE. N.E.

NOCHE

"Corn is an efficient way to get energy calories off the land and soybeans are an efficient way of getting protein off the land, so we've designed a food system that produces a lot of cheap corn and soybeans resulting in a lot of cheap fast food."
Michael Pollan

WILD RICE AND CHICKEN SOUP

Oak Grove Market not only offers custom-cut meats but also provides a wide selection of cooked foods, including complete meals, soups, sandwiches, salads and desserts to eat in or take out. Mark Maughon, co-owner of the market, was happy to scale down this soup so you can enjoy it at home.

2 skinless, boneless chicken breasts
3 C. low-sodium chicken broth
1 C. water
2 tbsp. butter
1 C. sliced celery
½ C. coarsely shredded carrot
½ C. chopped onion
½ C. chopped green bell pepper
3 tbsp. all-purpose flour
1 tsp. salt
¼ tsp. pepper
1½ C. cooked wild rice
1 C. half and half
⅓ C. sliced almonds, toasted
¼ C. chopped parsley

1. In a pot, cover chicken with broth and water and bring to a simmer. Cook for 8-10 minutes, until chicken is just cooked through. Skim off any scum that appears on the surface and discard. Remove chicken from broth, let cool slightly and cut into bite-size cubes. Reserve broth.

2. In a stockpot, melt butter. Add celery, carrot, onion and green pepper and cook until softened, about 5 minutes.

3. Stir in flour, salt and pepper until blended. Add wild rice, chicken and reserved broth and stir to combine. Bring to a boil, cover and reduce to a simmer. Cook for 15 minutes, stirring occasionally.

4. Add half and half, almonds and parsley. Cook just until hot. Do not boil.

OAK GROVE MARKET
2757 LAVISTA ROAD

"Failen while I ate up your bait grain."
Chinese Proverbs

167

Signature Tastes of ATLANTA

The OK Cafe opened its doors July 8, 1987, and so great was the longing for a true Southern restaurant that by the end of the first week it had become an Atlanta phenomenon with crowds standing in line to get in. Today it serves more customers than any other full service restaurant in Georgia.

¼ C.(½ stick) butter
1 medium onion, sliced lengthwise
1 ham hock
1 qt. water
1 tbsp. sea salt
1 tsp. ground white pepper
1 lb. honey
5 lb. collard greens, washed, stems removed, and chopped into 1-inch pcs. (or use a 3-lb. bag of pre-washed and stemmed collard greens)

1. In a large stockpot or Dutch oven, melt the butter over medium-high heat.

2. Add the onion and ham hock and cook, stirring constantly, until onions become translucent, 5 to 7 minutes.

3. Add the water, salt, pepper and honey and bring to a boil.

4. Add the collard greens and return to the boil.

5. Reduce heat to maintain a low simmer and cook until tender, about 1 hour and 45 minutes.

1284 W. PACES FERRY ROAD

OK CAFE

"The difference between involvement and commitment is like ham and eggs. The chicken is involved; the pig is committed."
Martina Navratilova

Pan-Seared Diver Scallops, Baby Beets and Greens with Truffle Honey Vinaigrette

Located on the main floor of the historic space, Parish serves a variety of Southern inspired dishes with modern twists, alongside a classic fully stocked raw bar, six nights a week. Saturdays and Sundays boasts an impressive comfort food inspired brunch.

1 lb. red or golden beets with green tops attached
1 tsp. and 1 tbsp. olive oil, divided
Kosher salt and freshly ground black pepper
1 sprig rosemary
1 tbsp. white balsamic vinegar
1 tbsp. honey, preferably orange blossom
3 tbsp. olive oil
1-1½ tsp. freshly cracked black pepper
truffle oil, to taste
6 diver or sea scallops

1. Preheat oven to 400°F.

2. Wash and dry beets and greens well. Chop greens, measure 2 cups and refrigerate, discarding excess or save for another use. Place beets in aluminum foil, drizzle with 1 tsp. olive oil, sprinkle with salt and pepper and place rosemary on top. Tightly seal and roast for 45 to 60 minutes, or until beets are fork tender. Set aside to cool; remove skins and cut into wedges.

3. Meanwhile, in a bowl or container, combine the vinegar and honey and drizzle in 3 tbsp. oil. Season to taste with pepper and truffle oil. Set aside.

4. In a skillet over medium-high heat, add the 1 tbsp. of oil. Season the scallops on both sides with the salt and pepper. Sear scallops for 3 minutes per side.

5. While scallops are cooking, mix reserved greens and beets with just enough vinaigrette to lightly coat and adjust seasonings. In the center of 2 plates, place 3 seared scallops and garnish with the dressed greens and beets.

Parish Foods and Goods
240 N Highland Avenue Northeast

"Scallops are expensive, so they should be treated with some class. But then, I suppose that every creature that gives his life for our table should be treated with class."
Jeff Smith

PEAR CRUMBLE TART

Executive Chef Robert Gerstenecker, known for his flair in creating contemporary dishes, uses the finest seasonal ingredients available from Atlanta and around the globe. Tasting menus are favorites at dinner, where classic meets contemporary. The concise wine list is primarily American, with a focus on red varieties and many boutique labels.

Sugar Dough:
½ C. (1 stick) unsalted cold butter, diced
¼ C. granulated sugar
1 egg yolk
2 C. all-purpose flour

Sour Cream Pear Filling:
1½ C. sour cream
½ C. granulated sugar
4 tbsp. all-purpose flour
1 egg
1 tsp. vanilla extract
pinch salt
5 ripe pears, peeled, cored and sliced ⅛-inch thick

Streusel:
½ C. (1 stick) cold butter, diced
½ C. packed light brown sugar
½ C. granulated sugar
1 C. all-purpose flour
1 C. whole oats

For the Sugar Dough:
1. Preheat oven to 350°F.
2. In a mixing bowl fit with the paddle attachment, cream butter and sugar together, allowing some lumps to remain.
3. Add yolk and mix until combined. Add flour and mix until smooth.
4. Turn out dough onto plastic wrap, flatten into a disc and, if very soft, chill until firm. The dough will be crumbly at first but should hold together. Roll out to ¼-inch thickness and cut to fit into a 10-inch tart pan or press with fingertips directly into the pan (you will have extra dough).
5. Bake tart shell for 15-20 minutes, or until lightly colored. Set aside to cool.

For the Sour Cream Pear Filling:
1. In a medium bowl, combine sour cream, sugar, flour, egg, vanilla and salt.
2. Add pears and toss gently to coat.
3. Spoon pear mixture into the tart shell, mounding pears slightly in the center.

For the Streusel:
1. In the same mixing bowl used for crust, combine the butter and sugars. Mix until crumbly.
2. Gradually add flour and mix until incorporated. Add oats and mix until combined.
3. Top pear mixture with streusel (you will have extra streusel).
4. Bake for 35-45 minutes or until streusel and crust are golden.

PARK 75 AT FOUR SEASONS HOTEL
5 14TH ST. N.E.

"It is, in my view, the duty of an apple to be crisp and crunchable, but a pear should have such a texture as leads to silent consumption."
Edward Bunyard

POLLO ALLA SCARPARIELLO

Located in the heart of the prestigious Dunwoody Village, Peter's has a beautiful, yet relaxed atmosphere for your dining pleasure or to celebrate any special occasion. Reward your taste buds with crisp salads, rich seafood, tender veal steaks, fresh pastas and fine wines. Our personable servers will strive to provide you with the very best experience.

peanut oil for frying
1 whole fryer chicken, cut into pcs.
1 potato, peeled and diced
6 oz. Italian sausage (about 2 links), sliced into rounds
6 mushrooms, sliced
8-10 pepperoncinis, chopped
1 tbsp. non-pareil capers
16 Kalamata olives, halved
4 cloves garlic, minced
2 tsp. dried oregano
1 C. chicken broth
2 tbsp. fresh chopped basil

1. Preheat oil in the fryer to 360°F.

2. Fry the chicken until browned and very crispy, about 20 minutes.

3. After 15 minutes, add the potatoes and cook 5 minutes. When the chicken and potatoes are done, drain briefly on paper towels.

4. Meanwhile, in a large skillet or sauté pan over medium heat, cook the sausage until it releases some of the fat, about 2 minutes.

5. Add the mushrooms and cook until browned, about 5 minutes. Add the pepperoncinis, capers, olives, garlic and oregano and cook a few more minutes. Add the chicken broth and bring to a simmer.

6. Add the chicken and potatoes to the pot. Turn the chicken until it is well coated in the sauce. Add the basil. Transfer to a platter and serve.

5592 CHAMBLEE DUNWOODY ROAD

PETER'S

"I do adore food. If I have any vice it's eating. If I was told I could only eat one food for the rest of my life, I could put up with sausage and mash forever."
Colin Baker

NEW ORLEANS BREAD PUDDING

For over 30 years, Petite Auberge has served fine French cuisine and Continental classics to a discriminating Atlanta clientele. Nestled away in a quiet corner of the Toco Hill Center, this Atlanta French restaurant keeps its guests coming back with such distinctive favorites as Beef Wellington, Coq au Vin, Rack of Lamb and many more.

1 C. (2 sticks) butter, melted
2 C. granulated sugar
8 French rolls, about 2 oz. each, one day old
1 C. raisins
2 C. half and half
7 eggs
2 tbsp. vanilla extract

Whiskey Sauce:
½ C. (1 stick) butter
1 C. granulated sugar
¼ C. whiskey (more if desired)

1. Preheat oven to 350°F.

2. Brush a little of the melted butter, about 2 tbsp., to grease a 9x13-inch baking pan. Coat the pan with a thin layer of sugar, about 2 tbsp.

3. Cut rolls into quarters or slices and arrange in the pan. Pour the remainder of the melted butter over the top of the rolls. Place raisins throughout the bread.

4. In a bowl, mix half and half, eggs, the remaining sugar and the vanilla. Carefully pour egg mixture over the rolls, making sure not to overflow. Cover the pan with foil and place in a water bath. Bake for 55-60 minutes, or until firm. Let the bread pudding sit for at least 30 minutes.

5. Meanwhile, make the whiskey sauce: In a medium skillet, melt butter and whisk in sugar until the sugar is completely dissolved. Add whiskey and blend well. Serve warm with bread pudding.

PETITE AUBERGE
2935 N. DRUID HILLS ROAD

"When you share your last crust of bread with a beggar, you mustn't behave as if you were throwing a bone to a dog. You must give humbly, and thank him for allowing you to have a part in his hunger."
Giovanni Guareschi

ASPARAGUS GAZPACHO

Portofino is an unassuming neighborhood bistro located on a quiet side street in Buckhead. From the street, you can see the beautiful stone and brick patio that offers the most enjoyable outdoor seating in town, The patio spills into a delightful dining room with vaulted ceilings, hardwood floors and bright, energetic artwork. The cuisine at Portofino is American-Italian offering a selection of simple pastas, innovative bistro-style appetizers and entrees. The menu and award winning wine list are constantly changing, the atmosphere is charged, and good times prevail.

1 lb. fresh asparagus, tough ends removed
½ lb. leek tops (medium to dark green parts only), rinsed well
1 large green bell pepper, seeds and white membrane removed
¼ C. tightly packed fresh basil
4 cloves fresh garlic
¼ C. freshly grated parmesan cheese
½ C. cold water
1 tsp. seasoned salt
1 tsp. sea salt or Kosher salt
1 tsp. freshly ground black pepper
½ C. best-quality extra virgin olive oil
½ C. champagne vinegar or white wine vinegar

1. Bring a pot of water to a boil. Blanch asparagus for 20-30 seconds, until it turns very bright green, and then immediately shock it in ice-cold water.

2. In a blender or food processor (working in batches if necessary), puree the asparagus, leek tops, bell pepper, basil, garlic, parmesan cheese and water until the soup is well combined and smooth.

3. Add the seasoned salt, sea salt, pepper, olive oil and vinegar and pulse to combine. Adjust seasonings as desired and chill until ready to serve.

PORTOFINO BISTRO
3199 PACES FERRY PLACE

"Wine makes every meal an occasion, every table more elegant, every day more civilized."
Andre Simon

GRILLED LAMB CHOPS
WITH MUSHROOM FUNGHETTO

A contemporary Italian restaurant with a creative menu, dramatic interior and friendly service, Pricci is fun, stylish dining at its best. Casual and classy, Pricci was named one of America's "20 Best New Restaurants" the year it opened by Esquire and called "…a dazzlingly modern, very hip Italian restaurant." The innovative menu combines classic cuisine with modern flair. The result is a wide array of salads, pasta, pizza, meats and desserts that will dazzle with every bite.

1 C. crushed Italian tomatoes
¼ C. extra virgin olive oil
2 tbsp. fresh lemon juice
1 tbsp. whole-grain mustard
¼ C. fresh rosemary, roughly chopped
3 garlic cloves, minced
1 tsp. salt
½ tsp. ground black pepper
6 thick-cut Frenched rib lamb chops
1 tbsp. butter
9 oz. wild mushrooms
¼ C. veal jus

1. In a 9-inch square baking dish, combine the tomatoes, olive oil, lemon juice, mustard, rosemary, garlic, salt and pepper and whisk until well combined.

2. Dip the lamb into the marinade to coat. Cover and marinate the lamb in the refrigerator overnight.

3. Preheat a grill to medium-high heat.

4. In a sauté pan over medium-high heat, melt the butter and add mushrooms and sauté until tender, 4 to 5 minutes.

5. Wipe off extra marinade from the chops and grill to desired doneness, about 3 minutes per side for medium-rare.

6. Arrange half the mushrooms on each of two plates. Top with three lamb chops each. Drizzle each with half the veal jus.

PRICCI
500 PHARR ROAD

"Try the mustard, —a man can't know what turnips are in perfection without mustard."
Mark Twain

KEY LIME PIE

Enjoy breathtaking views of Centennial Park and the Atlanta skyline while experiencing exquisite menu items from around the world. Our contemporary design showcases an open kitchen exhibition grill, hearth oven, and floor-to-ceiling wine rack.

Graham Cracker Crust:
1¼ C. graham cracker crumbs
3 tbsp. granulated sugar
5 tbsp. butter, melted

Pie Filling:
4 egg yolks
2 tsp. very finely grated lime zest
2 tsp. very finely grated lemon zest
1 (14-oz. can) sweetened condensed milk
¼ C. Key lime juice (if using bottled Key lime juice use ½ C.)
pinch salt

Pie Topping:
½ C. heavy whipping cream
2 tbsp. confectioners' sugar
1 tsp. combination of lemon and lime zest
splash vanilla extract
splash almond extract

For the Graham Cracker Crust:
1. Preheat oven to 350°F.
2. In food processor, pulse graham crackers and sugar.
3. Add butter and pulse until incorporated.
4. Line a 9-inch pie pan with crumb mixture, packing firmly. Bake pie shell for 5 minutes, or until golden brown.
5. Remove from oven and let cool.

For the Filling:
1. Whip egg yolks, lime and lemon zest until yolks take on a pale green color.
2. Beat in condensed milk and lime juice.
3. Scrape the sides and bottom of bowl for even mixing. Add salt and mix to combine.
4. Pour mixture into cooled crust and return to oven.
5. Bake for 10-15 minutes, or until edges are firm and the center (about the size of a half-dollar) is still soft and jiggles.
6. Allow to cool at room temperature and refrigerate for 4 or more hours.

For the Topping:
1. With an electric mixer, beat cream, confectioners' sugar, lemon-lime zest and vanilla and almond extracts to firm peaks. Using a spatula spread the cream on top of the chilled pie.

PRIME MERIDIAN
100 CNN CENTER

"Even when people are rich and successful on TV shows, there's always some trouble—you have to poke holes in them, throw them out of a job, put a pie in the face."
Drew Carey

MILLET CORN CASSEROLE

R. Thomas Deluxe Grill is a family-owned and operated restaurant located right on Peachtree Street in the Brookwood neighborhood of Atlanta, Georgia. Established in 1985 as a funky burger joint with a little healthy California style flair, R. Thomas has evolved into a landmark in the Atlanta restaurant culture, expanding the menu to include a broad variety from fresh to order juices and smoothies, free-range meats and organics, vegetarian and vegan, macrobiotic, gluten free, and raw food items as well breakfast anytime.

Signature Tastes of ATLANTA

2 tbsp. organic, unrefined cold pressed coconut oil or organic ghee (clarified butter)
1 large yellow onion, diced
⅛ tsp. crushed dried red pepper flakes
2 tsp. cumin
1 tbsp. Celtic brand sea salt or Herbamare
1½ tbsp. Spice Hunter brand Spicy Fajita Seasoning or Frontier Herbs brand Mexican Seasoning
6 C. water
2 C. organic millet grains, washed and drained
½ C. amaranth grain, washed and drained
2 C. fresh or frozen corn
1 large red bell pepper, diced

1. In large pot heat the coconut oil over low heat.

2. Add onion and crushed red pepper flakes and sauté until onion is softened and lightly browned.

3. Stir in cumin, sea salt and fajita seasoning and sauté for 3-5 minutes.

4. Add water, millet and amaranth and bring to a boil, stirring well. Cover and reduce heat to a simmer and cook for 15-25 minutes, or until grains are thick but not lumpy, stirring occasionally.

5. Fold in corn and return to a simmer. Fold in peppers and simmer 5 minutes. The mixture should be thick but not solid. Adjust seasonings to taste and remove from heat.

6. Preheat oven to 350°F.

7. Lightly grease a 9x13-inch casserole dish with coconut oil or ghee and pour mixture into pan. Bake for 30 minutes.

8. Check after 20 minutes and rotate for even cooking. Texture should be firm but not hard and top should be lightly browned.

R. THOMAS DELUXE GRILL
1812 PEACHTREE ST. N.W.

"A good marriage is like a casserole, only those responsible for it really know what goes in it"
Barbara Grizzuti Harrison

BANANA PEANUT BUTTER CREAM PIE

Signature Tastes of ATLANTA

Pastry:
1½ C. all-purpose flour
1 tbsp. granulated sugar
½ tsp. salt
½ C. shortening
¼ C. ice-cold water

Vanilla Cream:
2 C. heavy whipping cream
½ vanilla bean
1½ tbsp. cornstarch
3 tbsp. water
⅔ C. granulated sugar
6 large egg yolks (reserve whites for meringue)

Meringue:
6 large egg whites
1½ C. granulated sugar

Tarts or Pie Filling:
½ C. Skippy creamy peanut butter
2 bananas, sliced ¼-inch thick

8 (3½-inch) fluted tart shells or 1 (9-inch) pie pan

For the Pastry:
1. Preheat oven to 325°F.
2. Sift the flour, sugar and salt together in a mound. Using your fingers, crumble the shortening into the flour mixture until the shortening is in pea-size pieces.
3. Make a well in middle of the mixture and add the water; mix until the dough just comes together.
4. Wrap in plastic and refrigerate for 5 minutes.
5. Roll the dough out on a floured surface (or between 2 pieces of parchment paper) to about ⅛-inch thickness. Use a 4-inch ring cutter to cut out 8 circles and line the bottom and sides of the tart shells. (Alternately, use the whole sheet of rolled pastry to line a 9-inch pie pan.) Freeze for 10 minutes. Line the pastry with foil and fill with dry beans; bake for 30-45 minutes or until golden brown depending if you are using tart shells or 9-inch pie shell.

For the Vanilla Cream:
1. Place the cream and vanilla bean in a heavy saucepan and bring to a boil. Turn off the heat and let the bean steep for 30 minutes, then scrape the seeds from the bean and add the seeds to the cream.
2. Prepare an ice bath by nesting a dry bowl inside another bowl that is filled partway with ice water.
3. In a small bowl or cup, stir together the cornstarch and water and set aside.
4. Stir ⅔ cup sugar into the cream and return to a boil. Whisk a small amount of the hot cream into the egg yolks, and then whisk the yolk mixture back into the cream. Whisk the cornstarch mixture into the cream.
5. Cook until the mixture is thick and just starts to bubble on the sides, about 2 minutes.
6. Pour through a strainer into the bowl set in the ice bath. Let the vanilla cream cool to room temperature, stirring to bring the temperature down quickly. Refrigerate until needed.

For the Meringue:
1. Place the egg whites and sugar into the top of a double boiler set over boiling water.
2. Whisk the mixture until the sugar is dissolved and the temperature of the egg whites reaches 165°F.
3. Pour the hot whites into the bowl of a mixer with a whisk attachment and whip on high speed until the meringue is thick, stiff and cooled to room temperature. Place the meringue in a pastry bag fitted with a star tip.

To Assemble the Tarts or Pie:
1. Spread equal amounts of peanut butter into the tart shells or along the bottom of the 9-inch pie shell.
2. Arrange the sliced bananas on top of the peanut butter.
3. Fill the shell(s) to the top with the vanilla cream.
4. Pipe large stars of meringue in concentric circles over the surface of the vanilla cream or spoon meringue on top and smooth with a spatula. If desired, brown meringue with a propane torch.

RATHBUN'S
112 KROG ST., SUITE R

"Man is like a banana: when he leaves the bunch, he gets skinned."
Proverb

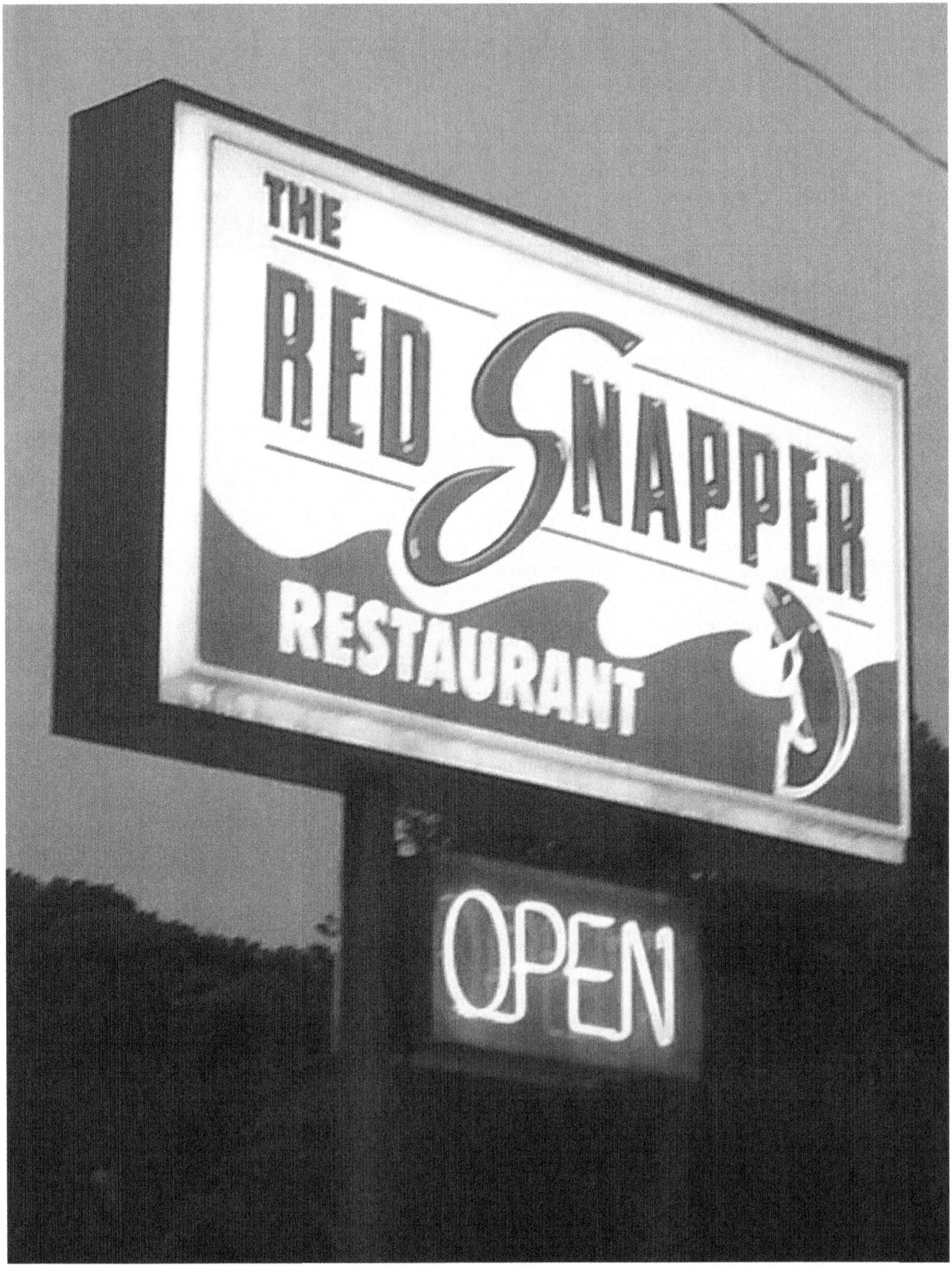
THE
RED SNAPPER
RESTAURANT
OPEN

OYSTERS SARA

Signature Tastes of ATLANTA

Spinach:
2 tbsp. butter, melted
3 tbsp. all-purpose flour
1 C. heavy cream
1 C. milk
1 tsp. granulated sugar
1 tsp. salt
½ tsp. Worcestershire sauce
½ tbsp. Tabasco sauce
¼ tsp. white pepper
¼ tsp. black pepper
1 (10-oz.) box frozen chopped spinach, thawed and drained
1 tsp. ground nutmeg
1 C. sliced mushrooms

Fried Oysters:
vegetable oil
½ C. white cornmeal
½ C. all-purpose flour
salt and pepper
18 oysters (fresh shucked or packaged)
½ C. milk

For the Spinach:
1. In a bowl, combine butter and flour to form a paste. Set aside.
2. In a heavy saucepan over medium heat, combine cream, milk, sugar, salt, Worcestershire sauce, Tabasco and white and black peppers, and bring to a light simmer.
3. Add spinach and nutmeg and mix well.
4. Add flour paste and mix to avoid clumps.
5. When completely blended, add mushrooms. Return to a simmer for 2-3 minutes.

For the Oysters:
1. Heat oil for a deep fryer to 350°F.
2. On a plate, combine cornmeal and flour and season with salt and pepper.
3. Dip oysters in milk, then coat with flour mixture.
4. Deep fry until golden brown (you might need to do this in batches; do not overcrowd).
5. Transfer the spinach to a small casserole dish or bowl. Top with fried oysters.

RED SNAPPER

2100 CHESHIRE BRIDGE ROAD

"Get action. Seize the moment. Man was never intended to become an oyster."
Theodore Roosevelt

WHITE CHOCOLATE FONDUE

The Ritz-Carlton, Atlanta is downtown's premier business address and a luxurious oasis in the heart of the city. Awe-inspiring interiors create an unequaled environment for work and play. Surrounded by the state's centers of finance and government, and just minutes from the Georgia Aquarium and sports events at the Georgia Dome, Philips Arena and Turner Field, this downtown Atlanta hotel is ideally situated.

2 lb. premium white chocolate
1 pt. heavy whipping cream
¼ C. honey

1. Chop the white chocolate into small pieces and put in a large bowl.

2. In a saucepan, stir together heavy cream and honey. Bring to a boil. Pour over the white chocolate and stir until all the chocolate melts.

3. Serve in a fondue pot to keep warm and offer a variety of fruits and other dippers.

Signature Taste of ATLANTA

RITZ-CARLTON BUCKHEAD
3434 PEACHTREE ROAD N.E.

"Chocolate is a perfect food, as wholesome as it is delicious, a beneficent restorer of exhausted power. It is the best friend of those engaged in literary pursuits."
Baron Justus von Liebig

HERBED CHEESE GRITS

Roman Lily Cafe is located in the recently revived Inman Park area, between Midtown and downtown Atlanta. The restaurant was opened by one of the former chefs at the Flying Biscuit Cafe, a popular area eatery. The American-style menu features eclectic variety, and includes hamburgers, sandwiches and steaks. The casual atmosphere tends to attract a funky city crowd.

6 C. water
2 C. stone-ground grits
2 tbsp. butter or butter substitute
1 tbsp. dried parsley
½ tbsp. garlic powder
1 tbsp. onion powder
1 tbsp. dried oregano
1 tbsp. dried basil
½ tbsp. paprika
½ tbsp. Kosher salt
½ tbsp. coarsely ground pepper
10 slices white American cheese (or more, to taste)
diced tomato for garnish, optional

1. In a large, heavy saucepan, bring the water and grits to a boil. Reduce heat to simmer.

2. Stir in butter or butter substitute.

3. Add dried parsley, garlic powder, onion powder, oregano, basil and paprika.

4. Cook for 20-30 minutes, stirring occasionally, until grits are soft and creamy.

5. Add salt, pepper and cheese, stirring until cheese is completely melted. Top with diced tomato, if desired.

ROMAN LILY CAFE
668 HIGHLAND AVE.

"Poets have been mysteriously silent on the subject of cheese."
G.K. Chesterton

Roxx Tavern is a casual neighborhood eatery that prides itself in offering high-quality fresh food and drink. Our turkey breasts are premium grade and roasted in-house. Our chargrilled steaks are the finest quality aged angus beef. Our wild Alaskan salmon is natural and sustainable. We hand-patty our award-winning black Angus beef burgers daily. Our delicious salad dressings and sauces are made in-house. All our desserts are bakery fresh. All for a very affordable price in a comfortable atmosphere.

6 tbsp. olive oil
½ lb. rutabagas, cut into large dice
½ lb. parsnips, cut into large dice
½ lb. carrots, cut into large dice
½ lb. shallots, halved
2½ lb. portobello mushroom caps, quartered
1½ tsp. minced garlic
1½ tsp. dried rosemary
1½ tsp. dried thyme
½ C. plus 2 tbsp. red wine
1 (16-oz.) can crushed tomatoes
2 C. mushroom stock (recipe follows)
¼ C. water
¼ C. all-purpose flour
1½ tsp. salt, or to taste
½ tsp. pepper, or to taste
1 tbsp. lemon juice

Mushroom Stock:
6 oz. portobello mushroom stems
1 unpeeled carrot, sliced
1 small leek, cut lengthwise
1 unpeeled small white onion, coarsely chopped
1 rib celery, sliced
1 clove garlic, unpeeled
1 sprig parsley
½ dried bay leaf
1 tsp. whole black peppercorns
¼ tsp. dried thyme
6 C. water

1. In a large Dutch oven heat the oil over medium-high heat. Add the rutabagas, parsnips, carrots and shallots. Cook, stirring frequently, until browned and caramelized, about 12-15 minutes.
2. Add mushrooms, garlic, rosemary and thyme. Cook 10 minutes, stirring occasionally.
3. Add the wine and stir to deglaze the pan.
4. Add the tomatoes and mushroom stock and bring to a boil. Cover, reduce heat to low and simmer for about 45 minutes.
5. In a small bowl, whisk together the water and flour. Stir into stew and cook, uncovered, for another 15 minutes, stirring frequently.
6. Season with salt, pepper and lemon juice. Serve at once or cool to room temperature and refrigerate.

For the Mushroom Stock:
1. In a small stockpot or Dutch oven, combine the mushroom stems, carrot, leek, onion, celery, garlic, parsley, bay leaf, peppercorns and thyme.
2. Add the water and bring to a boil over high heat. Reduce heat to low and simmer, uncovered, for about 1 hour, or until reduced by ⅓ to yield 4 cups.
3. Set aside 2 cups for the mushroom stew and reserve the rest for another use.

"Whatever dressing one gives to mushrooms, to whatever sauces our Apiciuses put them, they are not really good but to be sent back to the dungheap where they are born."
Denis Diderot

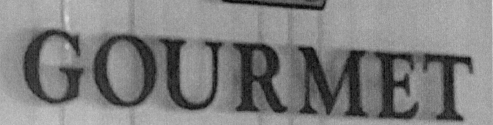

MANGO PUDDING

You will love the Chinese buffet at the Royal Gourmet in Marietta. This is a huge place, with a wide variety of Chinese food, lamb, yakitori, even sushi. This wonderfully simple dessert is called Mango Pudding and is a standout even among the many other dishes served at the international buffet. This dessert is from India.

Signature Tastes of ATLANTA

1 C. fresh mango slices
½ C. heavy cream
½ tsp. Grand Marnier
½ C. milk
2 (¼-oz.) packets unflavored gelatin
⅞ C. granulated sugar

1. Cut mango into small pieces and mash into a paste.

2. Stir in heavy cream and Grand Marnier. Set aside.

3. In a small saucepan, mix the milk and gelatin together.

4. Stir in sugar and heat gradually; do not let boil.

5. Remove from heat and slowly stir in the mango mixture.

6. Pour into 8 individual molds and refrigerate for 3 hours, or until set.

ROYAL GOURMET

4880 LOWER ROSWELL ROAD, SUITE 510-B

"The fact that it's such an aggressive beetle toward mango crops, and South Florida is the No. 1 mango growing area in the United States, we were very lucky to catch this.
Jennifer Connors

S&S
CAFETERIA
VISIT OUR FAST AND FRIENDLY TAKE OUT SHOP

★ **$6.59** ★

Meat
Two Vegetables
Bread & Butter

Guaranteed
Best Home-Style Food

99¢ Child's Plate
With Adult Meal

★ **$6.59** ★

SWEET POTATO BALLS

S&S Cafeteria offers their customers their choice of meals, with a selection of more than 115 items at each location. The company focus is to provide quality food and excellent customer service in all of its divisions which include: wholesale distribution and cafeteria dining. CEO J. A. Smith III grew up in the food business as his father founded the company. J. A. Smith Jr., Mr. Smith's father, was a veteran of the food service business before he opened the first S&S Cafeteria in Columbus, Georgia in 1936.

2½ lb. sweet potatoes
4 tbsp. (½ stick) margarine, melted
¾ C. plus 2 tbsp. granulated sugar
1 egg
2 tbsp. vanilla extract
12 oz. cracker crumbs, divided
6 large marshmallows, halved
1 slice of pineapple, cut into 12 pieces
salt, to taste
oil for deep frying

1. Preheat oven to 400°F.

2. Wash sweet potatoes well. Place in oven and cook about 50 minutes until very tender when pierced with the tip of a knife. When cool, peel and cut out any dark spots.

3. Place sweet potato pulp in bowl of a mixer and beat until smooth. Add melted margarine, sugar, egg, vanilla and 6 ounces of cracker crumbs, mixing well.

4. Divide mixture into 12 equal portions (a No. 12 scoop works well) and shape into balls. Roll balls in remaining 6 ounces of cracker crumbs. Place balls on tray and refrigerate 2 hours.

5. Heat deep fryer to 350°F. Place balls into hot oil and fry about 3 minutes, or until crispy and brown.

6. Garnish each with a bit of pineapple and ½ a marshmallow held in place with a toothpick.

Signature Taste of ATLANTA

2002 CAMPBELLTON ROAD SOUTHWEST, ATLANTA

S&S CAFETERIA

"A potato can grow quite easily on a very small plot of land. With molecular manufacturing, we'll be able to have distributed manufacturing, which will permit manufacturing at the site using technologies that are low-cost and easily available."
Ralph Merkle

Tomato, Basil and Eggplant Flatbread with Blue Cheese

Seasons 52 is a fresh grill and wine bar that invites guests to discover the sensational flavors of a seasonally-inspired menu and award-winning international wine list in a casually-sophisticated ambiance.

Signature Tastes of ATLANTA

1 recipe Flatbread Dough (recipe follows)
extra virgin olive oil (in a spray bottle)
1 tbsp. garlic, minced and lightly sautéed (or roasted garlic paste)
½ C. grated parmesan cheese
1 recipe Roasted Eggplant Slices (recipe follows)
1 bunch fresh basil leaves, torn
2 plum tomatoes, sliced very thin
½ C. crumbled blue cheese
freshly ground black pepper

Flatbread Dough:
1 C. water, warm to the touch (110-115°F)
1 tsp. granulated sugar
¼ tsp. active dry yeast
4 tsp. extra virgin olive oil
1 C. all-purpose flour
1½ C. whole-wheat flour, plus extra for kneading and rolling dough
1 tsp. salt
½ tsp. freshly ground black pepper

Roasted Eggplant Slices:
1 large eggplant, sliced about ⅛-inch thick
olive oil (in a spray bottle)
salt and freshly ground black pepper, to taste

For the Flatbread Dough:
1. In a measuring cup, combine the water, sugar and yeast. Set aside until yeast is bubbly, about 5 minutes. Stir in olive oil. In a medium bowl, combine the all-purpose and whole-wheat flours, salt and pepper. Make a well in the center and pour in the yeast mixture. Stir with a wooden spoon to combine.
2. Turn out dough onto a lightly floured board or other work surface. With lightly floured hands, knead the dough for 8 to 10 minutes — adding more flour just when the dough sticks to your hands or work surface — until the dough is smooth.
3. Transfer the dough to a lightly oiled bowl. Cover with plastic wrap or a damp towel and set in a warm, draft-free place until doubled in size, 1-2 hours. Punch down dough and divide into 4 equal pieces. Knead each dough piece on a lightly floured work surface for 1 minute into a tight ball.
4. Set dough balls on an oiled tray and refrigerate, covered, for 20 minutes or longer. (Dough can be made up to 1 day in advance. Wrap each ball in plastic wrap and store in the refrigerator.)

For Flatbreads:
1. Place a pizza stone on the lowest rack of the oven and pre-heat oven to 500°F. On a lightly floured surface, press a ball of Flatbread Dough into a disc, then roll it in a thin circle about ⅛-inch thick. Transfer the dough to a lightly floured wooden pizza paddle. Spritz the dough with extra virgin olive oil and sprinkle with some cooked minced garlic (or roasted garlic paste). Sprinkle with 2 tbsp. parmesan cheese. Add 3 to 4 eggplant slices, then 6 or 7 torn fresh basil leaves. Add 2 to 3 tomato slices. Top with 2 tablespoons crumbled blue cheese and a few grindings of black pepper.
2. Spritz with a little more olive oil, then gently slide the dough off the wooden paddle and onto the pizza stone. Bake 4-6 minutes, until the crust is crisp and golden brown. Remove flatbread with the paddle onto a cutting surface and slice.
3. Repeat the process with the remaining three flatbread discs.

For Roasted Eggplant Slices:
1. Preheat oven to 375°F. Soak the eggplant slices in cold water for 5 minutes. Drain and pat dry with paper towels. Spritz 2 baking sheets with olive oil.
2. Arrange slices in a single layer on the sheets, and then spritz them with more oil. Season with salt and pepper. Roast for 10 minutes until lightly browned. Cool and reserve for use.

SEASONS 52
3050 PEACHTREE ROAD

"Botanically speaking, tomatoes are the fruit of a vine, just as are cucumbers, squashes, beans and peas."
Horace Gray

MISS RUBY'S SEAFOOD GUMBO

Signature Tastes of ATLANTA

4 tbsp. oil, divided
1½ C. diced onions
1½ C. diced green and red peppers
1 C. diced celery
1 tbsp. minced garlic
5 C. clam juice or fish stock
1 (28-oz.) can diced tomatoes
2 bay leaves
2 tbsp. lobster or clam base
2 tsp. white or black pepper
1½ tbsp. dried rosemary
1½ tbsp. dried thyme
1 tbsp. paprika
1 tsp. cayenne pepper
2 tbsp. butter
2 tbsp. all-purpose flour
2 tbsp. gumbo file powder
2 lb. assorted seafood, cut into bite-size pieces (including salmon, shrimp or catfish)

1. In a large stockpot heat 2 tablespoons of the oil over medium heat.

2. Add onions, peppers and celery and cook until softened 10-15 minutes, stirring frequently.

3. Add garlic and cook for 1-2 minutes.

4. Add clam juice, bring to a boil, reduce heat and simmer for 10-15 minutes.

5. Add tomatoes, bay leaves, fish base, white pepper, rosemary, thyme, paprika and cayenne.

6. Bring to a boil, reduce heat and simmer for 10-15 minutes.

7. In a separate pan, melt the butter. Add flour and stir to combine. Cook 1-2 minutes, stirring constantly until totally combined.

8. Add mixture to stockpot and stir to combine. Bring to a boil, reduce heat to a simmer for 10-15 minutes until thickened, stirring frequently.

9. Add gumbo file powder and stir to combine. Simmer for 10 minutes while preparing the seafood.

10. In a separate large skillet, add the remaining oil. Gently sauté the seafood until just cooked. Add to the gumbo and stir gently.

SHARK BAR
571 PEACHTREE ST.

"The only kind of seafood I trust is the fish stick, a totally featureless fish that doesn't have eyeballs or fins."
Dave Barry

shorty's

HBORHOOD E

Shorty's is a neighborhood restaurant specializing in fresh, homemade food prepared in an authentic wood fired oven. The menu offers a variety of thin crust pizzas that can be made with toppings of your choice or ordered from our house specialty pizzas.

1¼ tsp. (about 1 clove) freshly crushed garlic
2 tsp. freshly crushed shallots
2 tbsp. balsamic vinegar
2 tbsp. sherry vinegar
1 tbsp. Dijon mustard
fresh ground pepper
pinch of salt
¾ C. olive oil blend (80/20) or pure olive oil

1. In a food processor or blender, puree the garlic and shallots.

2. Add the vinegars, mustard, pepper and salt.

3. With the motor running, slowly add the oil to emulsify.

4. Cover and refrigerate until ready to serve.

2884 N. DRUID HILLS ROAD N.E.

SHORTY'S

"Hatred, for the man who is not engaged in it, is a little like the odor of garlic for one who hasn't eaten any.
Jean Rostand

CHICKEN AND DUMPLINGS

Ruth Meadows Siler is a fixture in her Stone Mountain community. Extremely active at Stone Mountain First United Methodist Church, she has traveled the world, yet still returns to the delicious simple food she has prepared for over 80 years. Most importantly, she gave a young man a strong belief in himself and his ability to make something of himself. This recipe is the most requested of her repertoire.

4 large chicken breasts, bone-in and skin on
onion salt, to taste
celery salt, to taste
water
2 tbsp. white vinegar
1 (15-oz.) can evaporated milk
1 C. (2 sticks) salted butter

Dumplings:
2½ C. all-purpose flour
4 tbsp. Crisco shortening
1 egg, beaten
1½ C. buttermilk

1. Place chicken breasts into a heavy-bottom braising pan and cover with water. Add celery salt and onion salt to taste. Heat to a simmer and cook, uncovered, for 30 minutes.

2. Meanwhile, make the dumplings. Clear a large work area on a countertop and sprinkle generously with flour.

3. In a large mixing bowl, cut the Crisco into the flour until the dough resembles course meal.

4. Add the egg and buttermilk to the flour mixture and gently knead with your fingertips until the dough comes together.

5. Turn the dough out onto the floured surface and roll to ¼-inch thickness, then cut into 1-inch wide strips.

6. When the chicken is finished cooking, remove from the broth, debone and skin the chicken. Discard skin and bones. Shred the chicken and set aside. Reserve the broth.

7. Return the broth to the same heavy-bottom pan and heat to boiling. Add the vinegar and evaporated milk.

8. Slowly add the dumpling strips, tearing into 2-inch long pieces. Cook for 10 minutes, stirring gently to keep dumplings from sticking.

9. Add the butter and reserved chicken and simmer for 10 minutes. Allow to cool and enjoy.

CULINARY MENTOR AND LIFE INSPIRATION FOR THE AUTHOR

RUTH MEADOWS SILER

"If God had intended us to follow recipes, He wouldn't have given us grandmothers..."
Linda Henley

CHOCOLATE BREAD PUDDING WITH CLEAR CARAMEL SAUCE

Serving fresh, seasonal, all-American food in a stylish environment, Soho has been a neighborhood favorite for over 14 years. An American Bistro located in historic Vinings, Soho serves a menu bursting with delectable flavors inspired by many cuisines. Soho offers a progressive wine list and creative cocktails, as well as new wine and tapas pairings each week. Swift, attentive service, an award-winning wine bar and open kitchen all contribute to the high-energy buzz of Soho.

Signature Tastes of ATLANTA

1 qt. heavy whipping cream
1 lb. (about 7 slices) fresh breadcrumbs
11 oz. bittersweet chocolate, finely chopped
8 egg yolks
½ C. granulated sugar
2 tsp. vanilla extract

Clear Caramel Sauce:
1⅓ C. granulated sugar
1 C. water, divided

For the Pudding:
1. Preheat oven to 325°F. Bring a tea kettle of water to a simmer. Lightly coat an 8x12-inch or 9x13-inch pan with butter; set aside.
2. In a saucepan, heat the cream over medium heat until it comes to a low boil. Remove from heat.
3. Meanwhile, place the breadcrumbs and chocolate in a large mixing bowl and set aside.
4. In a separate mixing bowl, beat the egg yolks with the sugar. Whisk in a small amount of the heated cream, then whisk the egg yolk mixture into the hot cream. Whisk in the vanilla extract.
5. Pour the cream mixture over the breadcrumbs and chocolate and stir until the chocolate is melted.
6. Transfer to the prepared pan. Place the pan in a larger baking dish and pour the simmering water into the outer pan, about 1-inch up the sides. Bake the bread pudding in the water bath for 30-40 minutes, until set in the center. Serve warm with vanilla ice cream and warm caramel sauce.

For the Clear Caramel Sauce:
1. Combine sugar and ½ C. water in a heavy saucepan. Cook over high heat, swirling occasionally to dissolve sugar, and bring to a boil. Boil until the liquid turns caramel in color, 5-10 minutes. Carefully add remaining ½ cup water and swirl to dissolve. Transfer mixture to a heat-resistant glass or ceramic bowl. Cool slightly before serving, or cool to room temperature and then reheat a few seconds in microwave before serving.

4300 PACES FERRY ROAD S.E.

SOHO

"There is nothing particularly wrong with salmon, of course, but like caramel candy, strawberry yogurt, or liquid carpet cleaner, if you eat too much of it you are not going to enjoy your meal."
Lemony Snicket

CUCINA ITALIANA

DUCK RAGU WITH PAPPARDELLE

Signature Taste of ATLANTA

When Riccardo Ullio opened Sotto Sotto, he envisioned a restaurant serving all of the delicacies from his childhood. Twelve years later, the cozy, authentic Italian spot in historic Inman Park has been named Atlanta's Best Italian Restaurant by Bon Appetit, the Atlanta Journal-Constitution, CitySearch, Atlanta Magazine and AOL Cityguide. The focus of Sotto Sotto's kitchen is the creation of authentic Italian food with flavors developed from centuries of Italian culinary traditions, from Carnaroli rice risotto to a whole roasted fish.

4 duck legs and thighs
2 tbsp. extra virgin olive oil
1 medium yellow onion, chopped into ¼-inch dice
1 medium carrot, peeled and finely chopped
1 rib celery, chopped into ¼-inch dice
2 garlic cloves, thinly sliced
1 C. red wine (Chianti preferred)
1 (28-oz. can) San Marzano peeled whole tomatoes
1 C. chicken stock or broth
2 stalks rosemary, leaves only
salt and freshly ground black pepper
1½ lb. fresh pappardelle pasta (or 1 lb. superior quality dried)

1. Wash the duck legs and pat dry with paper towels. In a heavy-bottom Dutch oven or large saucepan, heat the olive oil until smoking. Add the duck legs and cook until brown on all sides, about 10-12 minutes.

2. Remove the duck legs and pour off and discard the excess fat from the pan. Add the onion, carrot, celery and garlic and cook until softened, 7-9 minutes. Add the wine, tomatoes and liquid, chicken stock and rosemary leaves and bring to a boil. Add the duck legs and return to a boil. Lower the heat, cover and simmer for 1 hour.

3. Remove the duck legs and allow to cool. Pull all the meat off the bones and return to pot (discard the skin and bones). Simmer, uncovered, for 30 minutes, or until sauce has thickened. Season with salt and pepper.

4. Before serving, bring a large pot of salted water to boil. Cook the pappardelle according to package directions until tender. Drain the pasta; add the warm sauce and toss to coat.

SOTTO SOTTO
313 N. HIGHLAND AVE. N.E.

"This desperate attack has more holes than a pasta strainer. This is another paid attack by union critics."
Sarah Clark

211

STUFFED CHICKEN BREASTS

Souper Jenny is a cozy neighborhood cafe open 6 days a week (unless we're tired and cranky and need an Attitude Adjustment Day). We traditionally offer six hot soups, two sandwiches and two to four salads a day! Favorites include "My Dad's Turkey Chili," Chicken Tortilla, Souper Power Green, Ripe Avocado Pita, The Club, Big Greek Salad and Chef Jessica's Broccoli Slaw. We have gluten free, vegetarian and vegan offerings every day!

Signature Taste of ATLANTA

2 tbsp. olive oil
2 sprigs fresh rosemary, chopped
zest of one lemon (about 2 tsp.)
8 skinless, boneless chicken breast halves
salt and pepper
1 (8-oz.) log goat cheese
1 (12-oz.) jar fire-roasted red peppers, drained and divided into 8 portions
1 bunch arugula

1. In a shallow dish, combine the olive oil, rosemary and lemon zest.

2. Place the chicken breast halves in the dish and turn them to coat completely in the oil mixture.

3. Marinate in the refrigerator for at least 2 hours, turning occasionally.

4. Preheat grill. Salt and pepper both sides of the chicken breast halves. Grill the chicken until cooked through but still juicy and tender, about 5 minutes per side. Remove from the grill and let cool 5 to 10 minutes.

5. With a sharp knife, slice each chicken breast in half horizontally, but do not cut completely through. Divide the goat cheese evenly and spread in the cavities of the chicken. Stuff each with a portion of the red peppers, and then top the red peppers with a few arugula leaves.

SOUPER JENNY
56 E. ANDREWS DRIVE N.W.

"Business is never so healthy as when, like a chicken, it must do a certain amount of scratching around for what it gets."
Henry Ford

CORN PUDDING

Signature Tastes of ATLANTA

Located in the heart of Midtown since 1993, South City Kitchen is proudly celebrating over 17 years of serving fresh and contemporary new Southern cuisine – with a sophisticated spin. Our award-winning food, wine list and service come together seamlessly for lunch, dinner or brunch.

10 ears corn, kernels removed, divided
2½ C. heavy cream, divided
1 (15¼-oz.) can corn, drained
5 eggs
¼ C. all-purpose flour
3 tbsp. granulated sugar
1¼ tbsp. baking powder
1 poblano chile or 1 jalapeño, seeded and diced
salt and pepper, to taste

1. Preheat oven to 325°F.

2. In a saucepan, combine half the fresh corn and cream and bring to a boil. Set aside.

3. In a food processor, place the remaining fresh corn and canned corn and puree.

4. In a large bowl, beat the eggs. Add the pureed corn, flour, sugar and baking powder. Stir in the chile. Stir in creamed corn mixture until combined. Season with salt and pepper.

5. Pour into a large casserole or 9x13-inch baking dish at least 2 inches deep. Cover with a piece of lightly oiled foil and bake in a water bath for 40-50 minutes or until just firm in the center. Remove from water bath and serve immediately.

SOUTH CITY KITCHEN
1144 CRESCENT AVE.

"Her corn-cake, in all its varieties of hoe-cake, dodgers, muffins and other species too numerous to mention, was a sublime mystery to all less practised compounders."
Harriet Beecher Stowe

Signature Tastes of ATLANTA

Star Provisions is the culinary dream shop for the gourmet expert and novice alike. Imagine having access to the pantry and walk-in cooler of Bacchanalia for your cooking preparations. That's what Star Provisions is all about! Featuring individual markets for cheese, wine, beer, meats, seafood and other gourmet food items, gifts and cookware, this is the place to buy the highest quality products including fresh cut meats, fish, foie gras, cheese (over 200 variations), freshly baked breads and sweets. Expect the highest level of service and knowledge.

1 C. unsalted Plugra butter, very cold and cut into chunks
½ C. granulated sugar
2 C. all-purpose flour, plus extra for flouring rolling surface and pin
1 pinch salt
1 pinch lemon, orange or lime zest (optional)

Icing:
2 egg whites
1 C. confectioners' sugar
food coloring (optional)

For the Cookies:

1. In a mixer set with the paddle attachment, cream butter and granulated sugar until wellcombined. Add flour, salt and zest, if using. Mix on low speed until combined.

2. Gather dough into a ball, wrap with clear plastic wrap, press to form a flat disk and chill at least 1 hour.

3. Preheat oven to 225°F. On a floured surface, roll out dough to ¼-inch thickness and cut out shapes with a favorite cookie cutter.

4. Place on cookie sheets and bake for 65 minutes. Remove cookies onto a rack and let cool completely.

For the Icing:

1. Mix egg whites and confectioners' sugar to spreading consistency.

2. Add food coloring, if desired.

3. Spread on cooled cookies.

4. Set cookies out on wax paper to dry completely, about 1 hour.

STAR PROVISIONS
1198 HOWELL MILL ROAD N.W.

"The Vice-Presidency is sort of like the last cookie on the plate. Everybody insists he won't take it, but somebody always does."
Bill Vaughn

STONEY RIVER FILET OSCAR

Stoney River is a place for legendary steaks, traditional favorites and creative flavors – in a classic lodge atmosphere, casual with contemporary style and flair, plus a staff that is friendly and engaging. Legendary steaks anchor the menu. Our Coffee-Cured Filet may become your personal favorite, or perhaps it will be our classic New York Strip or Bone-in Ribeye. Our Prime Burger is made with Gruyére cheese and caramelized onions. A dozen side dishes – mashed cinnamon sweet potatoes and three-cheese mac among them – add more flavors.

1 large bunch asparagus
4 (5-oz.) filets mignon
Kosher salt and freshly cracked pepper, to taste
2 tbsp. extra virgin olive oil
¼ C. (½ stick) unsalted butter
4 garlic cloves, chopped
1 lb. jumbo lump crab meat
1 C. Béarnaise Sauce (recipe follows)

Bearnaise Sauce:
2 tbsp. tarragon vinegar
2 tbsp. dry white wine
¼ C. finely chopped shallots
¼ tsp. ground black pepper, or to taste
1 tbsp. finely chopped fresh tarragon leaves, divided
3 egg yolks
½ C. (1 stick) unsalted butter, room temperature
salt and pepper, to taste

1. Preheat oven to 375°F. Bring a pot of water to boil. Blanch asparagus and set aside. Season beef with Kosher salt and cracked black pepper.

2. Heat olive oil in a cast iron or other heavy skillet. Sear filets for 3 minutes on each side. Transfer filets to the oven and cook to an internal temperature of 135°F (medium rare).

3. While filets are cooking, heat butter and garlic in a sauté pan. When butter is melted, add the asparagus, sprinkle with salt and pepper and heat through.

4. Heat crab meat in the microwave for 20 seconds; toss gently with the béarnaise. Place ¼ of the crab mixture atop each filet, and place ¼ of the asparagus on the side.

For the Bearnaise Sauce:
1. In a small saucepan over medium heat, combine vinegar, wine, shallots, black pepper and 1 teaspoon tarragon.

2. Cook until reduced to 1 tablespoon, 5-10 minutes.

3. Remove from heat. Add the egg yolks and 1 tablespoon water to reduced vinegar mixture. Whisk until thick and pale, about 2 minutes.

"One word, in this place, respecting asparagus. The young shoots of this plant, boiled, are the most unexceptionable form of greens with which I am acquainted."
William Andrus Alcott

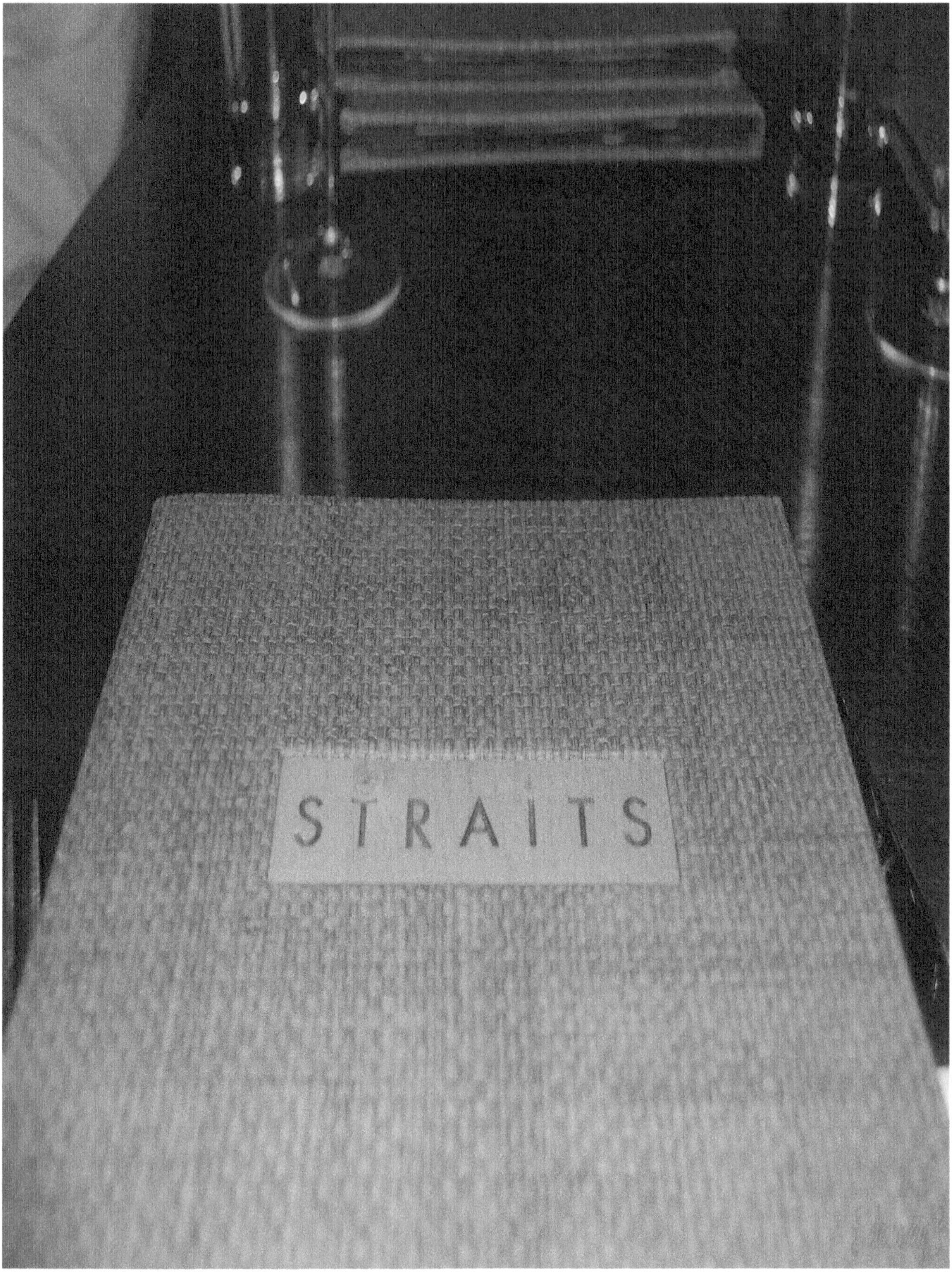
STRAITS

ORIGAMI SEABASS

The four major culinary cultures — Malaysian/Indonesian, Chinese, Indian and Nonya — are in fact, a blend of each other, creating a new cuisine that is unique and more complex in flavors and fragrances. Straits Restaurant offers a menu that includes all four Singaporean cuisine groups, plus a few others.

4 (6 oz.) filetsChilean
seabass
24 pcs. red bell pepper,
julienned
24 pcs. green bell pepper,
juliennes
12 Shiitake mushrooms,
juliennesd
48 pcs. ginger, julienned
36 pcs. dried longan
48 pcs. wolfberry
4 dashes white pepper
8 oz. origami sauce
2 tsp. sesame oil

1. Place the seabass in a pre-assembled parchment paper boxes.

2. Place even amounts of the peppers, mushrooms, ginger, longan, wolfberries, and pepper directly on top of the seabass in that order.

3. Pour 2 ounces of the origami sauce directly on top of the fish in each box then drizzle the sesame oil around the fish.

4. Put the top of the parchment box back on and microwave the seabass on high for 5 minutes.

STRAITS RESTAURANT
793 JUPITER STREET

"Mushrooms are like men--the bad most closely counterfeit the good."
Gavarni

CREAMY MUSHROOM SOUP

The Sun Dial Restaurant, Bar & View is Atlanta's only tri-level dining complex featuring a revolving upscale restaurant, a rotating cocktail lounge and an observatory View Level offering a breathtaking 360-degree panorama of the magnificent Atlanta skyline. An Atlanta tradition, thousands of locals and tourists board the scenic glass elevators each year to climb the hotel's 73 stories to The Sun Dial for its unbeatable views, classic cuisine, live jazz and relaxing ambiance.

1 oz. dried exotic mushrooms such as oyster, porcini, chanterelle, black trumpet or yellow foot
1 tbsp. olive oil, divided
2 tbsp. butter, divided
½ C. diced carrots
½ C. diced celery
½ C. diced onion
½ C. diced leeks
1 garlic clove, peeled and crushed
¼ lb. fresh crimini mushrooms, sliced in half or thirds
salt and pepper
¼ C. white wine, divided
1 qt. chicken stock (or vegetable stock), divided
4 oz. fresh shiitake mushrooms, sliced in thirds or quarters (discard stems)
1 C. heavy cream
dash of lemon oil

1. Place dried mushrooms in a bowl and cover with 1 cup hot water. Cover and set aside.
2. Lightly coat the bottom of a large soup pot with oil and add 2 teaspoons butter. On medium heat, sauté the carrots, celery, onion, leeks and garlic until vegetables are soft, about 7 minutes. Remove from heat.
3. Place vegetables in a blender or food processor with reconstituted dried mushrooms and soaking water and pulse to finely chop, but do not puree. Return vegetables to soup pot.
4. Lightly coat the bottom of a large sauté pan with oil and place over high heat. Heat the oil until very hot (the oil will shimmer), add 2 teaspoons butter and the crimini mushrooms. Sprinkle lightly with salt and cracked pepper. Do not stir. Allow to cook, untouched, until bottoms of mushrooms are golden (about 4-5 minutes), and then stir to turn. Allow to cook, stirring as little as possible, until the mushrooms are caramelized but not burned.
5. Deglaze pan with half of white wine. Place the cooked mushrooms in the blender with about ½ cup chicken stock and pulse until chopped but not pureed; add to soup pot. Repeat sautéeing, deglazing and blending process with the shiitake mushrooms.
6. Place pot with cooked vegetables and mushrooms over medium-high heat and add remaining stock. Simmer for 20 minutes.
7. While soup is simmering, place cream in a small pot and gently heat.
8. After soup has simmered for 20 minutes, slowly add cream. Season with salt, pepper and a dash of lemon oil.

"A soup like this is not the work of one man. It is the result of a constantly refined tradition. There are nearly a thousand years of history in this soup."
Willa Cather

THAI ICED COFFEE

Surin of Thailand has been serving Authentic Thai Cuisine since 1990 to Atlanta and the Southeast. First and second-generation customers have enjoyed our family recipes and regional dishes of Thailand. The experience of Authentic Thai Cuisine is coupled with a full Sushi Bar, a knowledgeable and professional wait staff, a full Martini Menu, varied wine list, and professional bartenders. Many of our Thai people are trained in Japan by professional Sushi Chefs and find an easy transition from our fresh, select, and "made to order" Thai Cuisine to our fresh, select, and "made to order" Sushi and Sashimi.

½ C. granulated sugar (or to taste)
5 C. freshly brewed coffee
1 C. half and half

1. Dissolve sugar in hot coffee.

2. Set aside to cool and refrigerate until cold.

3. Fill five large glasses with ice.

4. Fill each glass ¾ full with coffee and top with half and half.

SURIN OF THAILAND
810 N. HIGHLAND AVE.

"The morning cup of coffee has an exhilaration about it which the cheering influence of the afternoon or evening cup of tea cannot be expected to reproduce."
Oliver Wendell Holmes, Sr.

Frozen Fruit Salad

In 1965 a group of extraordinary women established the Forward Arts Foundation in Atlanta, Georgia. These distinguished arts patrons, whose dynamic leadership was matched by their determination, transformed the carriage house of the Swan House estate into a thriving restaurant, gift shop and art gallery.

6 oz. cream cheese, softened
¼ C. maple syrup
8 oz. whipping cream
1½ C. (20-oz. can) crushed pineapple, drained
½ C. chopped dates
½ C. chopped pecans

1. In medium bowl, beat cream cheese and maple syrup with a fork or electric mixer until well blended and fluffy. Set aside.

2. In another bowl, whip the cream until soft peaks form.

3. Add to the cream-cheese mixture to whipped cream and mix well.

4. Stir in pineapple, dates and pecans.

5. Spoon the mixture into an 8-inch square dish.

6. Cover and freeze at least 8 hours or until firm.

Swan Coach House
3130 Slaton Drive, N.W.

"Truth is a fruit which should not be plucked until it is ripe."
Voltaire

SWEET POTATO CUSTARD PIE

Located in the heart of Atlanta's historic Auburn Avenue, Sonja Jones's Sweet Auburn Bread Company is a small batch from scratch bakery serving homey, Southern-inspired desserts, breads and pastries. Home of the Sweet Potato Cheesecake ... fit for a President.

SWEET **A**UBURN **B**READ **C**OMPANY

234 AUBURN AVENUE NORTHEAST

Signature Tastes of ATLANTA

1 pie shell — either your favorite version or one found elsewhere

Pie Filling:
1 lb. sweet potatoes
1 C. sugar
1 tsp. fresh ground nutmeg
3 eggs
1/2 C. (1 stick) butter, melted
1½ C. half and half
1 tsp. vanilla extract
½ tsp. lemon extract

1. Preheat oven to 350°F.

2. Boil the sweet potatoes for 40-50 minutes, or until tender. Drain the potatoes, run under cold water, and remove the skin. Mash the potatoes in a mixing bowl and stir until smooth.

3. Stir in the sugar and nutmeg.

4. Add the eggs, one at a time, beating well after each addition.

5. Stir in the melted butter and half and half.

6. Stir in the vanilla and lemon extracts.

7. Pour the filling into the unbaked pie shell. Bake for 45-55 minutes, or until a knife inserted in the center comes out clean.

"The man who has nothing to boast of but his ancestors is like a potato — the only good belonging to him is under ground."
Sir Thomas Overbury

1280
table
RESTAURANT AND TAPAS LOUNGE

Sweet Potato Soup

Our inspired cuisine reflects regional flavors and attractive prices at lunch, dinner and brunch. Complimented by The Woodruff Arts Center's contemporary setting, our menus have all the ingredients to offer you a tasteful experience. We offer extensive selections, including specialty cocktails and award-winning wines to complement your dining choices.

1½ tbsp. unsalted butter
2 shallots, peeled and chopped
1 lb. sweet potatoes, peeled and chopped into 1½-inch cubes
4 C. chicken stock
1 C. heavy cream, divided
salt and pepper, to taste
cinnamon

1. In a medium saucepan over medium heat, melt the butter.

2. Add the shallots and cook until translucent, about 3 minutes.

3. Add the sweet potatoes and cover with the chicken stock. Simmer until the sweet potatoes are tender, about 20- 25 minutes.

4. Puree the mixture in a blender or food processor, then strain back into the saucepan over medium heat.

5. Add ½ cup cream and season to taste with salt and pepper.

6. To serve, whip the remaining cream. Add a dollop of whipped cream to each bowl, then pour the soup over it. Garnish with a dash of cinnamon.

Signature Tastes of ATLANTA

Table 1280
1280 Peachtree St. N.E.

"Money is the root of all evil, and yet it is such a useful root that we cannot get on without it any more than we can without potatoes."
Louisa May Alcott

OLD BAY CHICKPEAS

An rectangle-shaped bar floats in the middle of the ground floor with seating all around to frame the fact that at Tap, the drink is king. To add to the awe, each drinkable, whether wine or microbrew stored in kegs will float above guests' heads in a seventy-two barrel, glass-enclosed vault suspended from the top of the ceiling.

Signature Tastes of ATLANTA

1 lb. dried chickpeas
1 carrot, cut into thirds
1 stalk celery, cut into thirds
1 small onion, quartered
5 sprigs fresh thyme
2 cloves garlic, lightly crushed
vegetable oil for frying
Old Bay seasoning

1. In a large pot, cover the chickpeas with water, approximately double their volume. Let sit at room temperature overnight.

2. Drain the soaked chickpeas. Add the carrot, celery, onion, thyme and garlic, and cover with 1½ times their volume in fresh water.

3. Bring to a boil; reduce to a simmer and cook until tender but not falling apart, about 45 minutes.

4. Drain, remove the vegetables and thyme, and allow the chickpeas to dry slightly.

5. Heat the oil in the fryer to 325°F.

6. Fry the chickpeas until they are a dark golden color, crispy and light, about 5-8 minutes.

7. Drain on paper towels. Season with Old Bay. Serve slightly warm or at room temperature.

1180 PEACHTREE ST.

TAP

"A publisher who writes is like a cow in a milk bar."
Arthur Koestler

Taqueria Del Sol

AUTHENTIC MEXICAN TACO HOUSE

REFRIED BLACK-EYED PEAS

Signature Tastes of ATLANTA

1 lb. dried black-eyed peas
1 tomato
1 jalapeño
½ C. vegetable oil, divided
¼ medium onion, diced
2 garlic cloves, minced
8 oz. dry chorizo, diced
salt

1. Soak black-eyed peas overnight and cook according to package directions. Drain and set aside.

2. Preheat the broiler. Roast the tomato and jalapeño until charred, turning several times until evenly blackened. Rub with a little oil to soften, then puree in blender and set aside.

3. In a stockpot or large saucepan over medium heat, add remaining oil. Sauté onion, garlic and chorizo in oil until soft. Add cooked peas and tomato-jalapeño puree; cook until peas start to soften and break down (you can mash to get to desired consistency). Add salt to taste.

TAQUERIA DEL SOL
1200 HOWELL MILL ROAD NORTHWEST

"The federal government has sponsored research that has produced a tomato that is perfect in every respect, except that you can't eat it. We should make every effort to make sure this disease, often referred to as 'progress', doesn't spread."
Andy Rooney

The Tavern at Phipps is a see-and-be-seen bustling Buckhead hot spot. While the focus is on the classic American fare such as the famous Tavern Chips, crisp salads, fresh seafood and hearty pasta dishes, the energy of the bar always takes the cake. Consistently recognized for the "Best looking wait staff: bartenders: happy hour: outside patio: people watching spot and singles scene."

Nacho chips (enough to cover 2 plates)
½ lb. salmon chunks, cooked
½ lb. shrimp, cooked and peeled
8 oz. white American cheese, cubed
8 oz. heavy cream
½ C. diced red onion
¼ C. capers
¼ C. lobster base
1 tbsp. dill
⅛ tsp. chili powder
⅛ tsp. paprika

1. Heat the heavy cream, lobster base and cheese in a large sauce pan over medium heat, stirring constantly until mixture is completely melted.

2. Add onions and capers and simmer for 10 minutes until onions are soft.

3. Add salmon and shrimp, stir gently.

4. Add dill and chili powder, stir and remove from heat.

5. Put a layer of chips on an ovenproof plate, then add a generous helping of seafood mixture. Continue with a second layer.

6. Place under a broiler to brown.

7. Garnish with paprika and serve hot!

THE TAVERN AT PHIPPS
3500 PEACHTREE ROAD

"As the evening sky faded from a salmon color to a sort of flint gray, I thought back to the salmon I caught that morning, and how gray he was, and how I named him Flint."
Jack Handy

SMOKED SALMON CHIPS

Two Urban Licks has been heating up the Atlanta restaurant scene with its "Fiery American Cooking" and live music since opening in the fall of 2004. The one-of-a-kind experience available at Two Urban Licks has won over the Atlanta dining scene making it one of the city's busiest restaurants.

2 Idaho potatoes, scrubbed
vegetable oil for frying
dry spice seasoning, such as Tony Chachere's Creole Seasoning
Chipotle Cream Cheese (recipe follows)
8 oz. smoked salmon
1 small red onion, diced
2 oz. capers, drained
2 tbsp. chopped fresh chives

Chipotle Cream Cheese:
3 oz. (½ small can) chipotles in adobo sauce
1 (8-oz.) package cream cheese, at room temperature
juice of 1 lime
¼ C. chopped fresh chives
1½ tsp. coarse salt
1½ tsp. granulated sugar

Smoked Salmon Chips:
1. Preheat a fryer to 350°F.

2. Using a mandoline or a very sharp knife, slice the potatoes lengthwise 1/16-inch thick. Fry in oil on both sides until golden brown, about 3 minutes. Drain on paper towels. Sprinkle with seasoning. Cool to warm or room temperature.

3. To assemble, spread about 1 tsp. Chipotle Cream Cheese on one side of each chip. Top with a small piece of salmon (about ½ tbsp.). Sprinkle with red onion, capers and chives.

Chipotle Cream Cheese:
1. Place the chipotles and sauce in a food processor and puree until smooth. Add cream cheese and lime juice and process well. Scrape down sides of bowl.

2. Add chives, salt and sugar and pulse until well combined.

TWO URBAN LICKS
820 RALPH McGILL BLVD.

"If I had the choice between smoked salmon and tinned salmon, I'd have it tinned. With vinegar."
Harold Wilson

Signature Tastes of ATLANTA

Violette Restaurant was a dream-fulfilled for Guy Luck, a native of Strasbourg, France. He moved to the United States in the mid-1980's with the hope of opening his own café. All his life, Luck had been drawn to the United States. "I was always raised like we owed something to America for saving us during the war (World War II)," Luck once told an Atlanta reporter. So when he and his then girlfriend, Violette, decided to go their separate ways, Guy thought it as good a time as any to set out for a new life in the U.S.

1 lb. semisweet chocolate chips
6½ tbsp. unsalted butter, cut into pieces
6 eggs, separated
6½ tbsp. granulated sugar, divided
1 tbsp. vanilla extract
5 tsp. hot brewed coffee
2⅓ C. heavy whipping cream

1. In a double boiler over hot — but not boiling — water, melt chocolate chips and butter, stirring frequently. Remove from heat and set aside to cool.

2. Beat egg yolks with 3 tablespoons sugar and vanilla. Set aside.

3. Add coffee to chocolate mixture and stir until smooth. Add egg yolk mixture to chocolate and stir until smooth.

4. With an electric mixer, beat egg whites until stiff peaks form when beater is slowly raised. With a rubber spatula, gently fold egg whites into the chocolate mixture, using an under and over motion. Fold only enough to combine.

5. Add remaining 3½ tablespoons sugar to whipping cream and beat until peaks form when beater is slowly raised. Fold the whipped cream into the chocolate mixture, using a gentle under and over motion. Transfer to serving dish or individual bowls and refrigerate overnight.

VIOLETTE
2948 CLAIRMONT ROAD

"Eating chocolate can have significant influences on mood, generally leading to an increase in pleasant feelings and a reduction in tension."
Peter Rogers

241

VIRGINIA
RESTAURANT

LOUNGE

FETTUCCINE GORGONZOLA

The atmosphere is casual, the decor is inviting and classy with red brick columns, square amber wooden tables and hanging plants. They offer several dining areas including a patio with a bubbling fountain. For entertainment, there is live jazz every Thursday and dancing. They serve an eclectic American cuisine along with a breakfast menu that includes, Belgian waffles, pancakes, sausages and more. The bar serves beers, wines and cocktails.

Ingredients	Instructions
1 large unshucked ear of corn ½ lb. asparagus, cut into 2-inch pieces (tough ends discarded) 1 tbsp. olive oil 2 large shallots 2 tbsp. finely chopped chives ¼ C. white wine 2 C. half and half ½ C. crumbled gorgonzola cheese 1 tsp. cornstarch mixed in 1 tbsp. water salt and pepper, to taste 4 oz. sliced mushrooms 1 lb. fresh fettuccine 4 oven-dried tomatoes, or sun-dried tomatoes, thinly sliced ¼ C. shelled sunflower seeds ¼ C. grated parmesan cheese 2 grilled boneless chicken breasts, cut into thin strips 1 tbsp. chopped fresh parsley	**1.** Preheat the oven to 450°F. **2.** Roast corn in the oven until just tender, about 10 minutes. Cut off kernels and reserve. **3.** Meanwhile, bring a pot of water to a boil, blanch asparagus and set aside. **4.** In a pot heat the oil over medium heat. Add shallots and cook until translucent. **5.** Add chives and wine and stir to combine. **6.** Add half and half and gorgonzola and blend well. **7.** Add cornstarch mixture, salt and pepper. **8.** Add mushrooms, corn and asparagus and bring to a simmer. **9.** Cook pasta just until al dente, about 2-4 minutes. **10.** When vegetables are just cooked through, add pasta and toss well. **11.** Add dried tomatoes and toss again. **12.** Transfer to a serving bowl; garnish pasta with sunflower seeds and parmesan. Top with grilled chicken slices and sprinkle with parsley.

"Corn is an efficient way to get energy calories off the land and soybeans are an efficient way of getting protein off the land, so we've designed a food system that produces a lot of cheap corn and soybeans resulting in a lot of cheap fast food."
Michael Pollan

Signature Tastes of ATLANTA

Two brothers and a sister opened The Vortex Bar & Grill in Atlanta's Midtown neighborhood back in 1992 when the area was still underdeveloped. Considered to be a little family-owned corner pub, The Vortex soon earned a reputation for serving the best burgers in town and offering an excellent selection of booze. In addition to great food and spirits, the owners' off-beat humor and large collection of kooky décor became hallmarks of this new hangout. Because the siblings refused to tolerate what they called "jerks and idiots" in their establishment, The Vortex also gained notoriety for its unconventional, no-nonsense approach to customer service.

½ **lb. Monterey Jack cheese, shredded**
½ **lb. cheddar cheese, shredded**
6 oz. diced pimentos
¾ **C. mayonnaise**
½ **tbsp. salt**
½ **tbsp. white pepper**

1. In a bowl, mix cheeses, pimentos, mayonnaise, salt and pepper.

2. Press firmly into a container.

3. Cover and chill for 3 or more hours.

V ORTEX
438 MORELAND AVE.

"Dessert without cheese is like a beauty with only one eye."
Jean Anthelme Brillat-Savarin

Signature Tastes of ATLANTA

Yes, there really is a Bert! As a matter of fact, Bert has been with the Waffle House Inc. more than 30 years. He created his famous chili recipe in the early 1980's when he was working in Dallas, Texas. He tested several combinations before coming up with the perfect bowl of chili.

Twenty years later, Bert's Chili™ is still made to his exacting standards. Each pot of chili is prepared using only the finest ingredients, including chili beans, USDA Choice hamburger, Jimmy Dean sausage, tomato, onions and a special blend of seasonings.

2 (15-oz.) cans pinto beans (not drained)
1 lb lean hamburger
1/4 lb Jimmy Dean sausage
2 Cs. chopped yellow onion
1 can (15 oz.) tomato sauce
2 cubes beef bouillon (or 2 Tbsp beef bouillon granules)
1 tsp salt
1 tsp chili powder
3/4 tsp ground cumin
1/4 tsp black pepper
1/4 tsp sugar
1/8 tsp garlic powder
1/8 tsp ground oregano

1.   Brown hamburger, sausage and onions together in 6-quart saucepan.

2. Add pinto beans (not drained), add can of tomato sauce and add enough water to rinse can.

3. Add beef bouillon granules. If using beef bouillon cubes, dissolve in 1/4 cup water then add to the pan.

4. Add salt, black pepper, garlic powder, ground oregano, cumin, chili powder and sugar. Blend thoroughly.

5. Bring to boil, reduce heat and simmer for 15 minutes. Serve.

MULTIPLE LOCATIONS ACROSS THE CITY AND AMERICA

WAFFLE HOUSE

"I have always loved Waffle House. It's been like an oasis in the desert many times late at night after one of my concerts."
Trace Adkins

CORN PUDDING

Wisteria Restaurant is located in the historic Atlanta neighborhood of Inman Park. Housed in a building nearly a century old, our atmosphere is cozy and inviting. Our cuisine is contemporary American with a Southern twist sure to please every palate. Come in and enjoy Chef Jason Hill's seasonal menu featuring items such as All Natural Iron Skillet Fried Half Chicken and Molasses-Rubbed Pork Tenderloin. Wisteria prides itself on a diverse and extensive wine list served by a warm and knowledgeable staff.

Signature Tastes of ATLANTA

*1 C. rice flour
4 tsp. baking powder
½ C. granulated sugar
2 tsp. sea salt
2 lb. fresh or frozen corn
kernels (thawed if
frozen), divided
⅓ C. buttermilk
11 tbsp. butter, melted
2 eggs, beaten
1 C. shredded Asiago
cheese*

1. Preheat oven to 325°F.

2. In a large bowl, combine the rice flour, baking powder, sugar and salt. Set aside.

3. Place all but 1 rounded cup of corn kernels in a blender or food processor with the buttermilk; puree until smooth.

4. Stir pureed corn mixture into flour mixture. Add melted butter and eggs; stir until blended. Stir in Asiago and reserved whole corn kernels.

5. Spoon batter into a buttered 9x13-inch baking dish. Bake until lightly browned on top, 35-45 minutes. Cool slightly; cut into squares before serving.

WISTERIA
471 N. HIGHLAND AVE.

"Then plough deep while sluggards sleep, and you shall have corn to sell and to keep."
Benjamin Franklin

Signature Tastes of ATLANTA

"I should have no objection to go over the same life from its beginning to the end: requesting only the advantage authors have, of correcting in a second edition the faults of the first."
Benjamin Franklin

Steven W. Siler is a firefighter-cum-chef serving in Bellingham, Washington. Long marinated in the epicurean heritage of the Deep South, Steven has spent over 20 years (dear God has it been that long?!) in the much-vaulted restaurant industry from BOH to FOH to chef. In addition, he has served as an editor and contributing writer for several food publications. When not trying to shove food down his fellow firefighters' gullets, he enjoys sailing and sampling the finest of scotches and wines, and has an irrational love affair with opera. He swears one day he will relive the above picture on the Gulf Coast with a good Will.

The Signature Tastes series of cookbooks is the one of the first of a series of culinary celebrations from Smoke Alarm Media, based in the Pacific Northwest. Smoke Alarm Media is named for another series of unfortunate culinary accidents at an unnamed fire department, also in the Pacific Northwest. One of the founders was an active firefighter. Having been trained as a chef, he found himself in the position of cooking frequently at the fire station. Alas, his culinary skills were somewhat lacking in using the broiler and smoke would soon fill the kitchen and station. The incidents became so frequent that the 911 dispatch would call the station and ask if "Chef Smoke Alarm" would kindly refrain from cooking on his shift. Thus Smoke Alarm Media was born.

SIGNATURE TASTES

HIDDEN EATS

TABLE FACTS

BYGONE ERAS

ART OF CULINARY DIPLOMACY

VARSITY

SUBLIME NECTAR